WILLAMETTE VALLEY

BARBARA TRICARICO

SCHIFFER PUBLISHING

4880 Lower Valley Road • Atglen, PA 19310

Other Schiffer Books by the Author:
Oregon Coast, ISBN 978-0-7643-5947-7
Southern Oregon, ISBN 978-0-7643-5948-4
Central Oregon, ISBN 978-0-7643-5945-3

Library of Congress Control Number: 2020943547

Designed by Danielle Farmer
Cover design by Molly Shields
Front cover photo by Vdln Taylor
Back cover photos by Vldn Taylor and Charles Hillestad

Type set in BentonSans/Cambria

ISBN: 978-0-7643-6160-9
Printed in China

Published by Schiffer Publishing, Ltd.
4880 Lower Valley Road
Atglen, PA 19310
Phone: (610) 593-1777; Fax: (610) 593-2002
E-mail: Info@schifferbooks.com
Web: www.schifferbooks.com

INTRODUCTION

The lush Willamette Valley has a rich Native American history. Covered wagons once led emigrants over the 2,170-mile Oregon Trail from the Missouri River into Oregon.

Stretching 150 miles and encompassing over 750 vineyards and 500 wineries, this fertile land can be attributed to the Willamette River that flows through it, surrounded by mountains on three sides.

Gardens and flower farms produce a riot of color each spring and summer. The annual Wooden Shoe Tulip Festival in Woodburn is just one popular event held each spring. Not far away in Silverton is the beautiful 80-acre Oregon Gardens, which includes Oregon's only Frank Lloyd Wright structure, the Gordon House. Silver Falls State Park, near Silverton, is the largest in the Oregon State Parks system, covering more than 9,000 acres.

Salem, once a destination on the Oregon Trail, is the second most populated city in Oregon after Portland. It became the state capital in 1850.

No two colleges in Oregon are more competitive than the Beavers (Oregon State University in Corvallis) and Ducks (University of Oregon in Eugene). Since 1894, the two teams have competed in a popular annual football rivalry game.

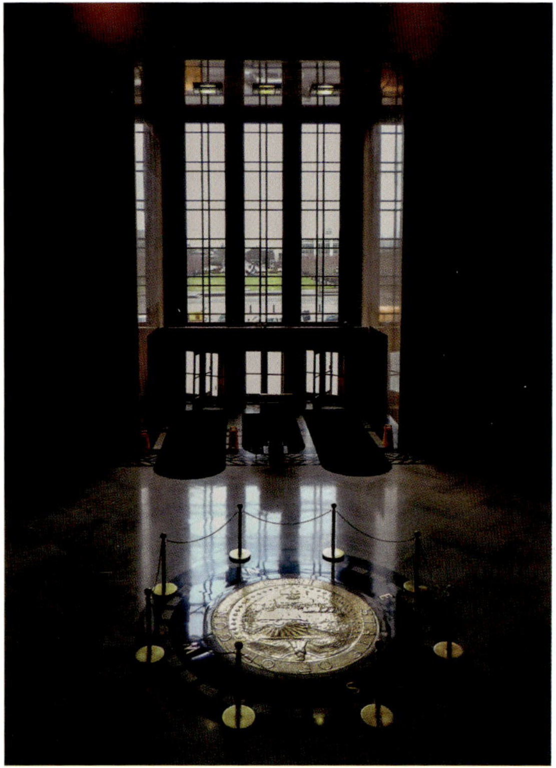

Salem State Capitol Rotunda, rebuilt in 1938. The original Oregon State Capitol was built in 1855 but was destroyed by fire twice. *Photo by Charles Hillestad*

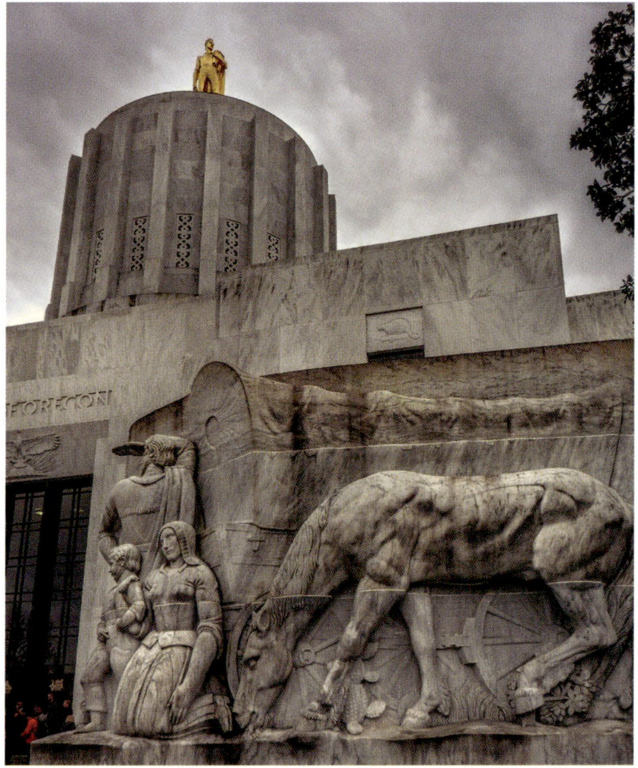

Salem State Capitol. Leo Friedlander's relief sculpture of pioneers, titled *Covered Wagon*, was created in 1934. *Photo by Charles Hillestad*

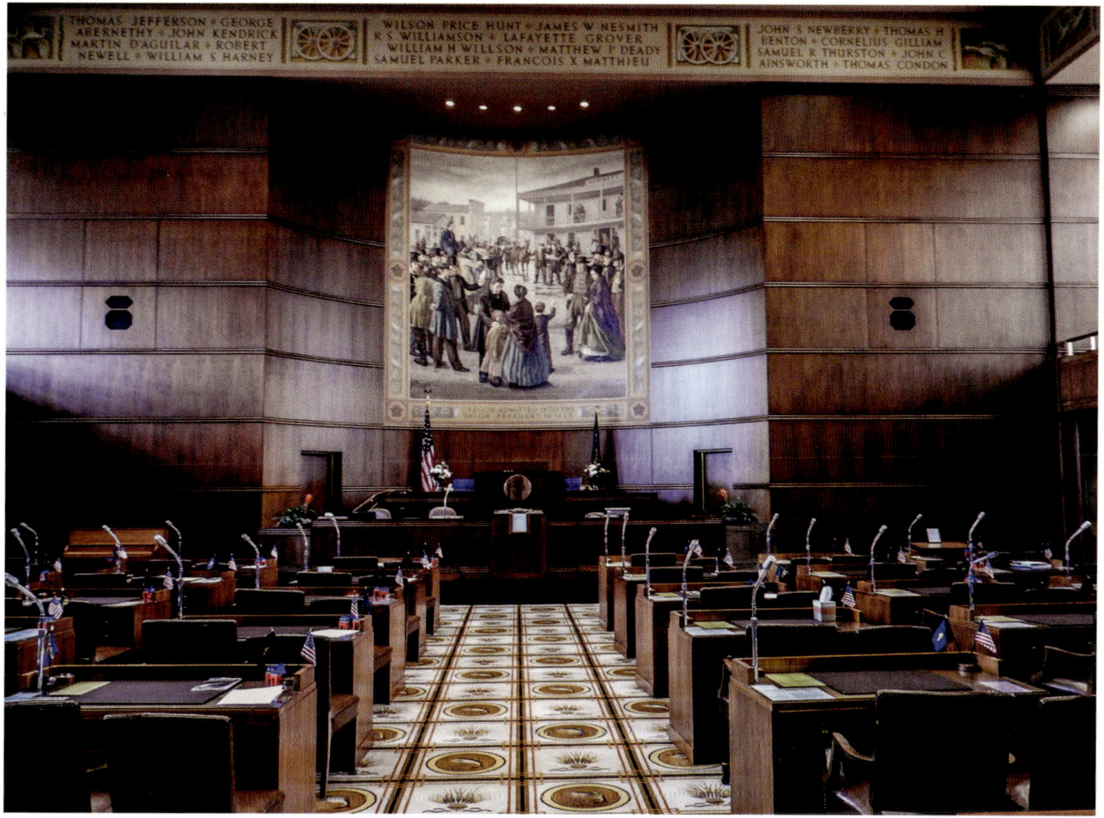

Salem State Capitol. State Senate Chambers. The mural depicting Oregon statehood was painted by Frank H. Schwarz. *Photo by Charles Hillestad*

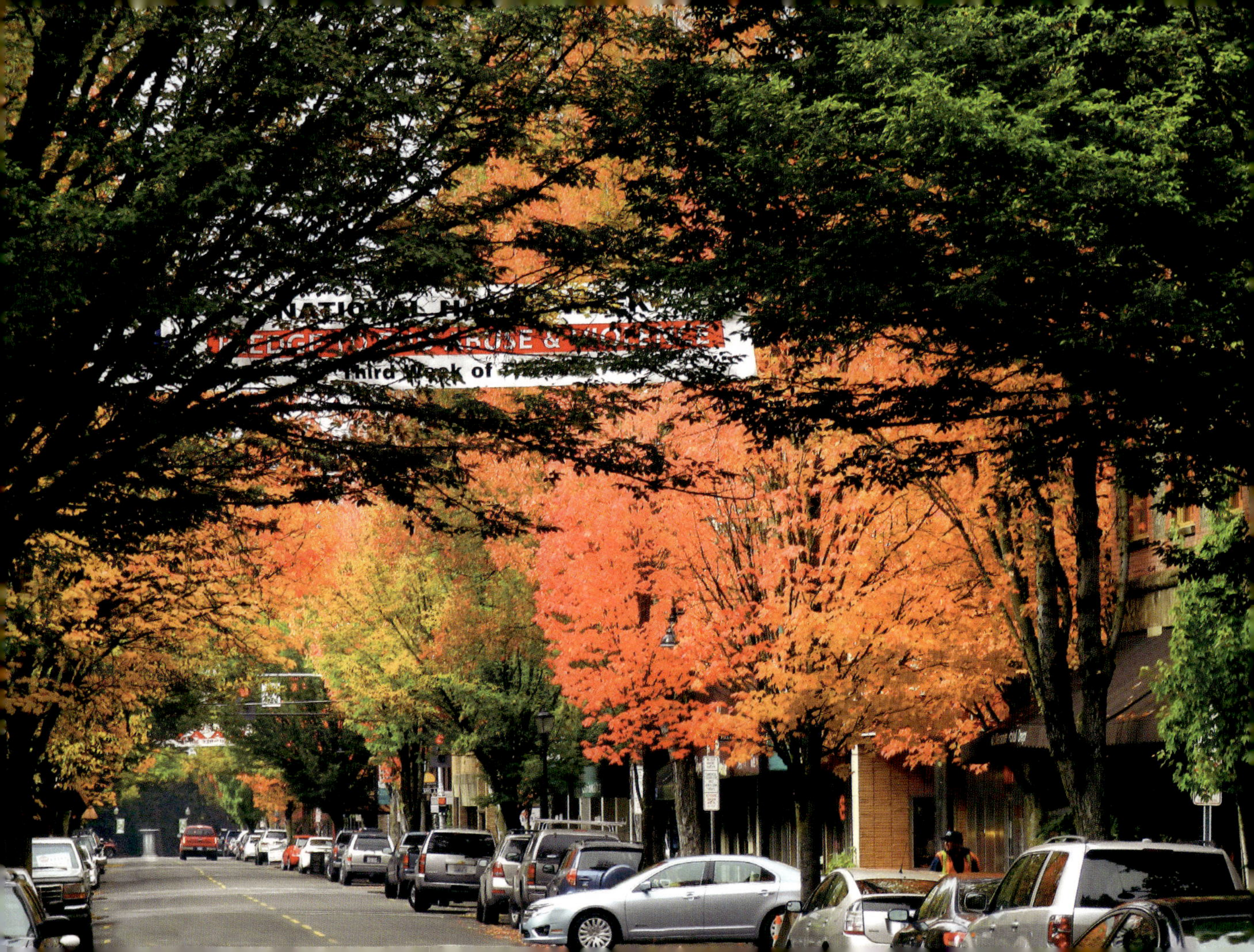

Downtown McMinnville's tree "tunnel."
Photo by Charles Hillestad

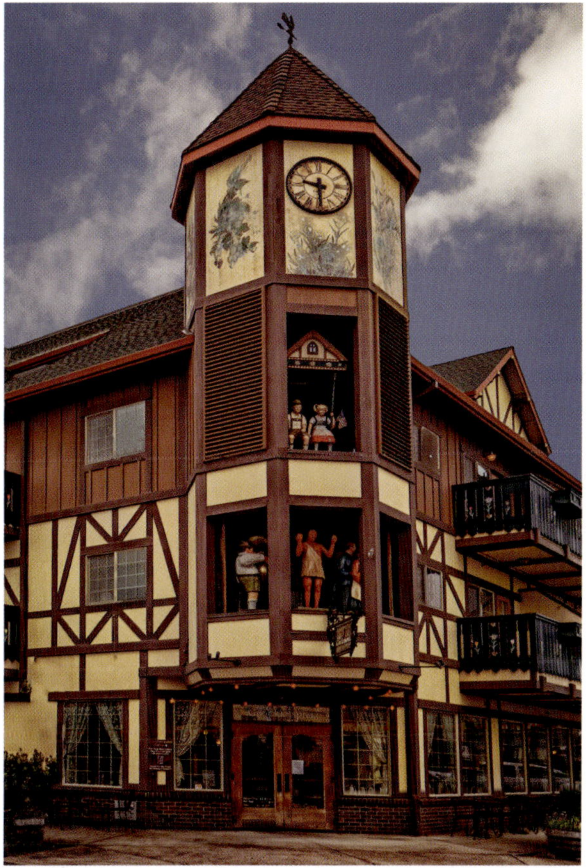

Glockenspiel, Mt. Angel. Seven carved wood characters circle four times daily at America's tallest glockenspiel. Each year, Mt. Angel holds an Oktoberfest celebrating its Swiss German heritage. *Photo by Barbara Tricarico*

Willamette Valley farm near Hopewell.
Photo by Charles Hillestad

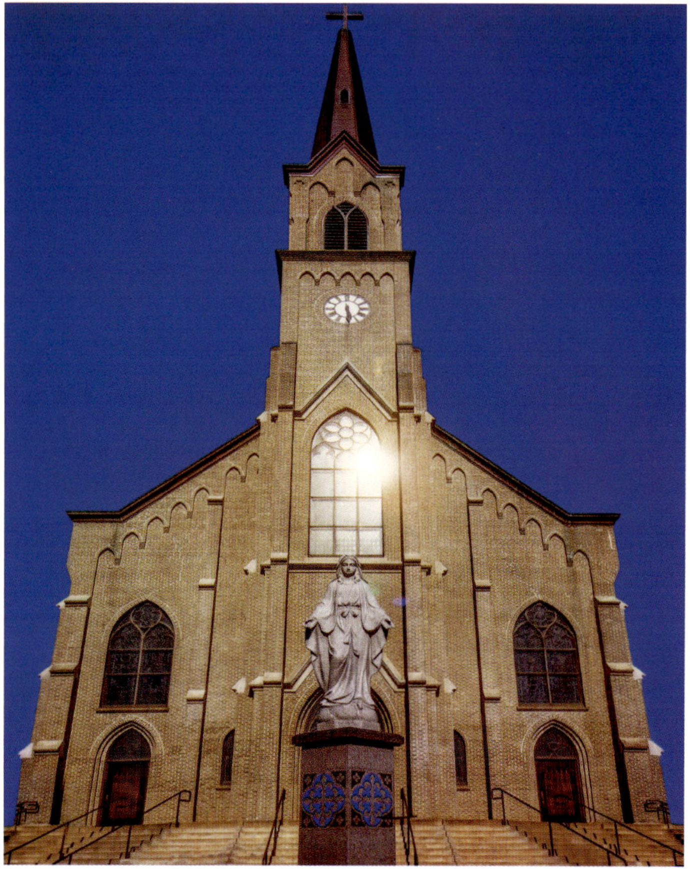

St. Mary's Church, Mt. Angel, built in 1912.
Photo by Cornelius Matteo

Interior, St. Mary's Church, Mt. Angel.
Photo by Barbara Tricarico

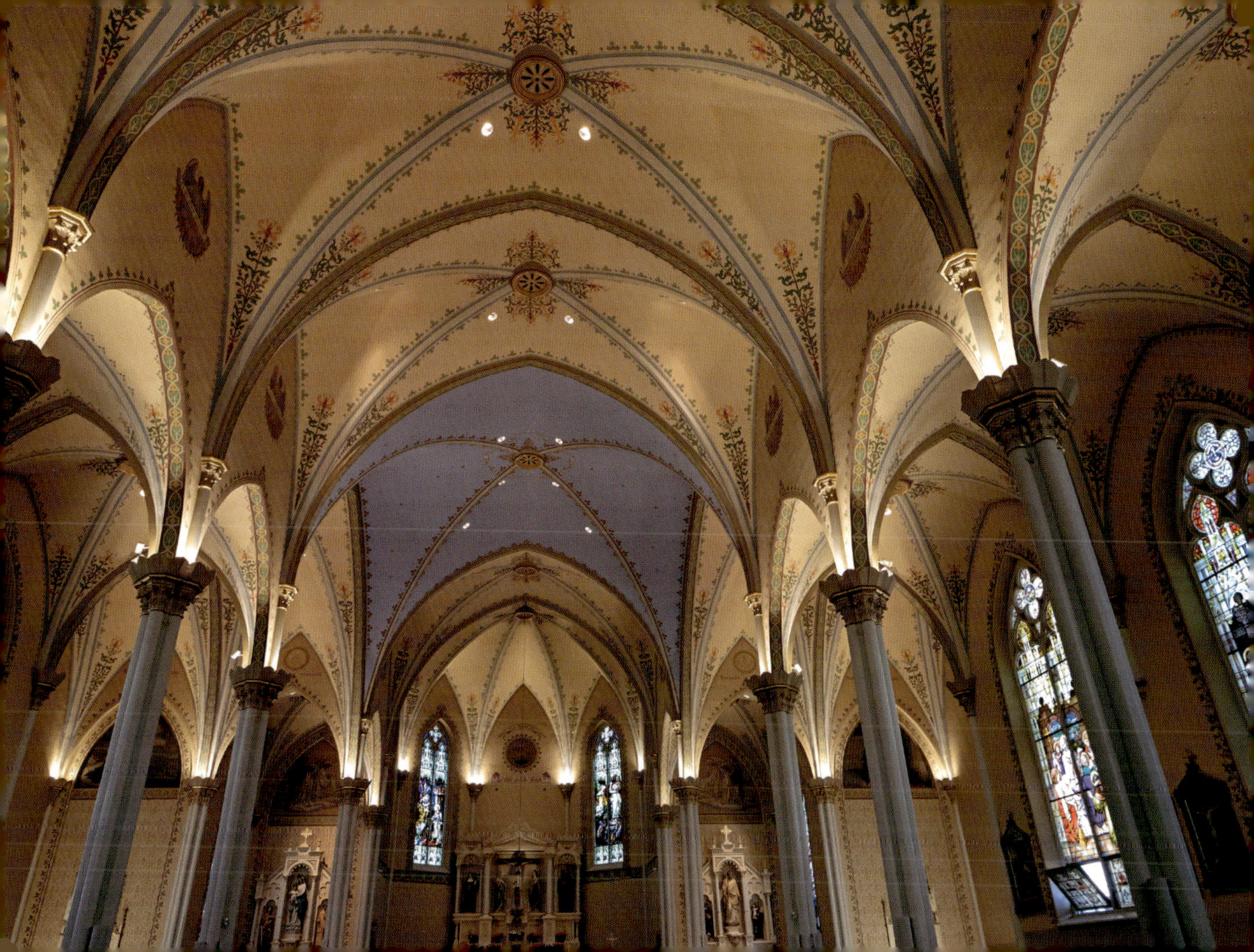

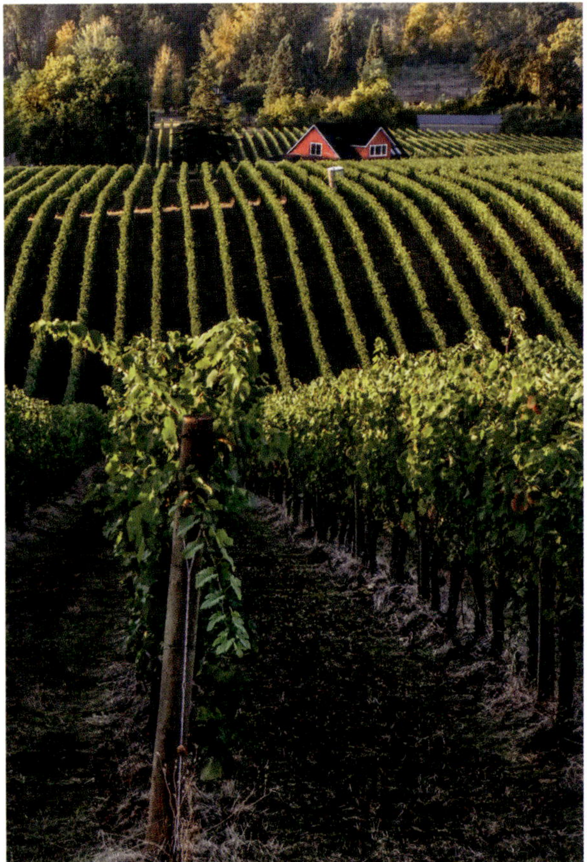

Farm and vineyard in Beaverton.
Photo by Neal R. Thompson

Willamette hilltop.
Photo by Charles Hillestad

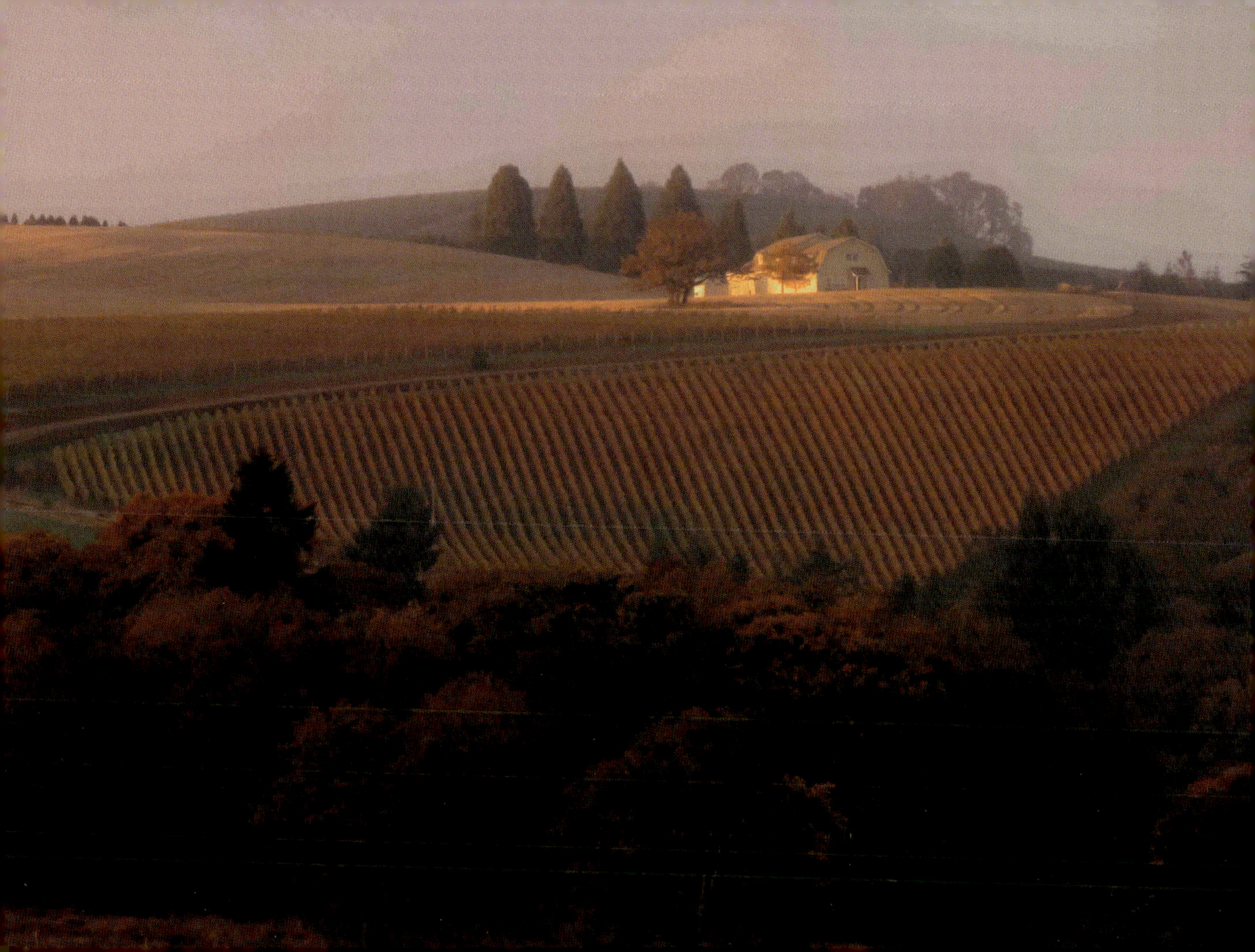

14

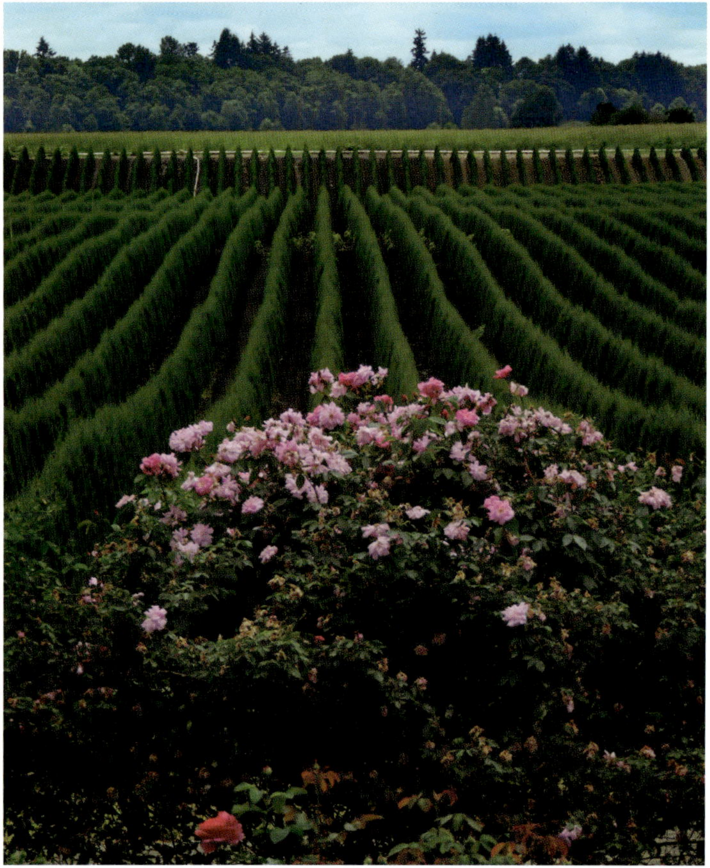

Heritage Rose Nursery near St. Paul.
Photo by Charles Hillestad

Swan Island Dahlia Festival, Canby.
Photo by Charles Hillestad

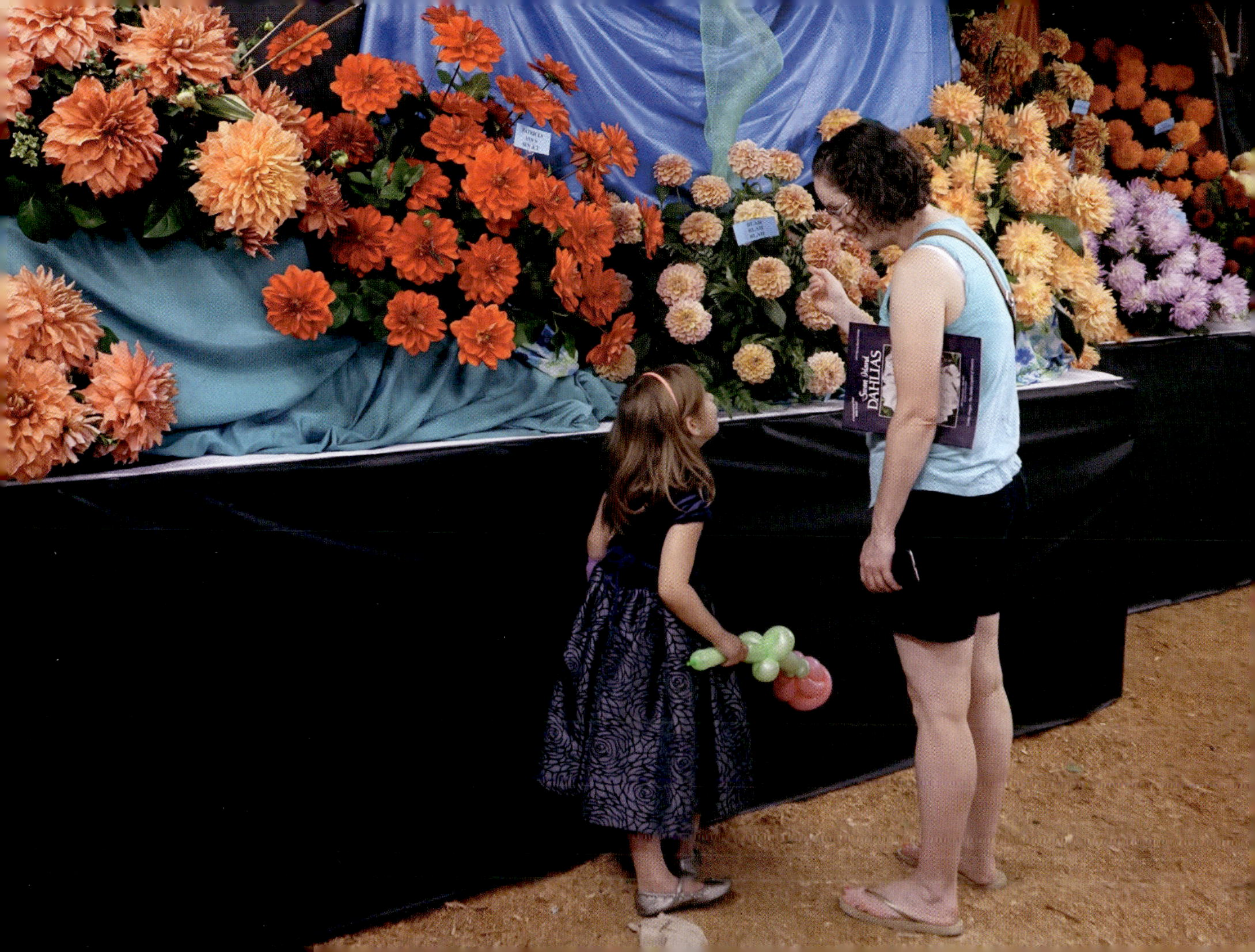
DAHLIAS

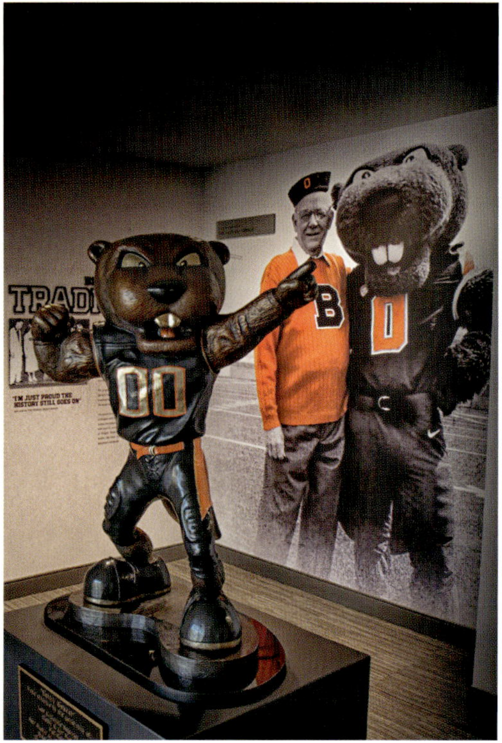

Benny the Beaver, Oregon State University's mascot, Corvallis. Ken Austin was the first Benny the Beaver mascot, in 1952. Bronze sculpture completed in 2017 by Oregon native Alison Brown. *Photo by Barbara Tricarico*

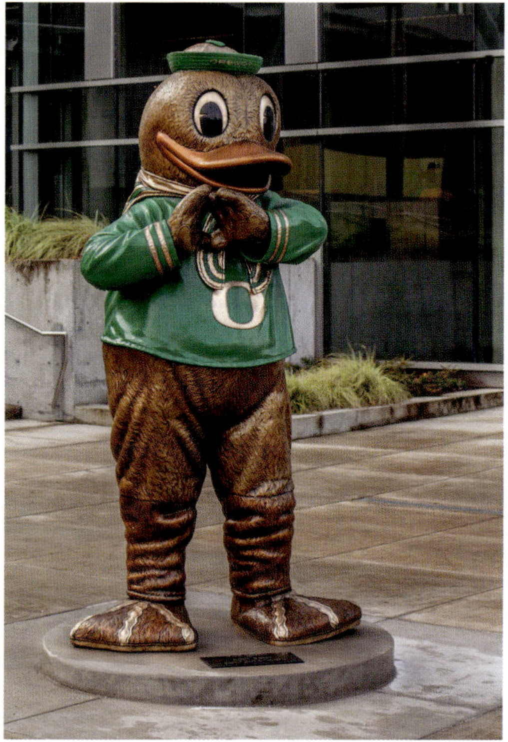

The Oregon Duck, University of Oregon's mascot. Bronze sculpture completed in 2016 by Alison Brown. *Photo by Ellen Ahern*

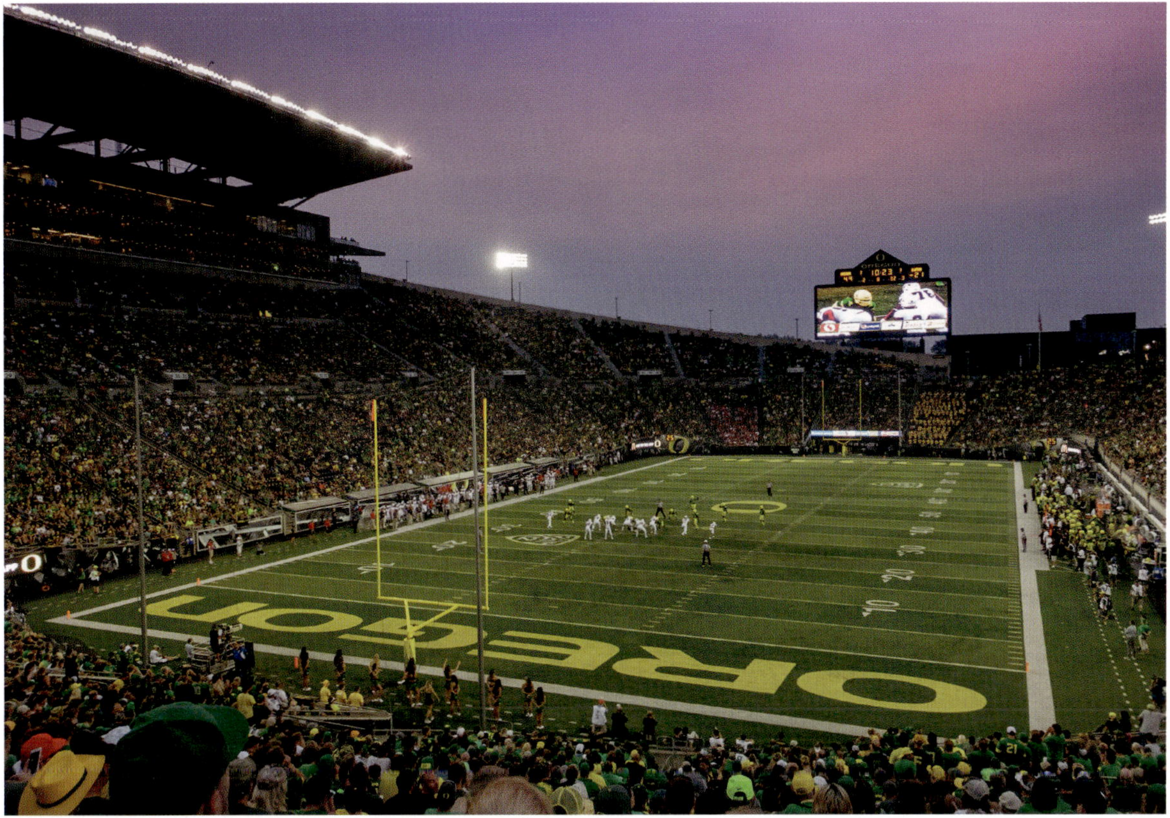

Autzen Stadium, University of Oregon, Eugene.
Photo by Bob Palermini

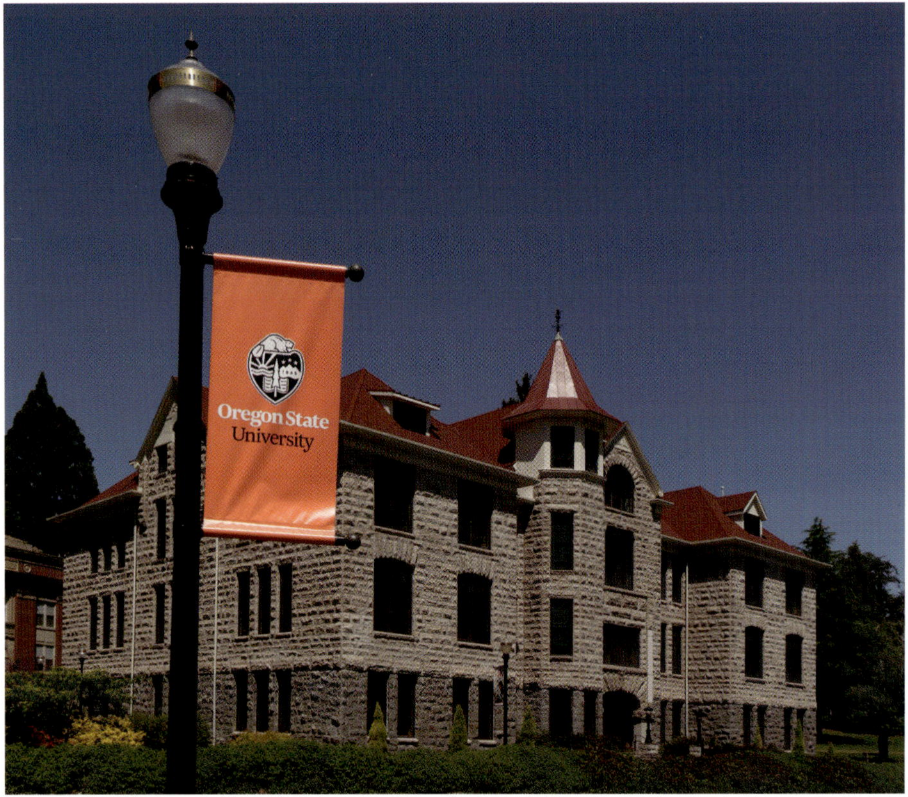

Education Hall, Oregon State University, Corvallis, designed by Charles H. Burggraf, dedicated in 1902. *Photo by Barbara Tricarico*

Lillis building complex, atrium ceiling, University of Oregon, Eugene, completed in 2003. *Photo by Barbara Tricarico*

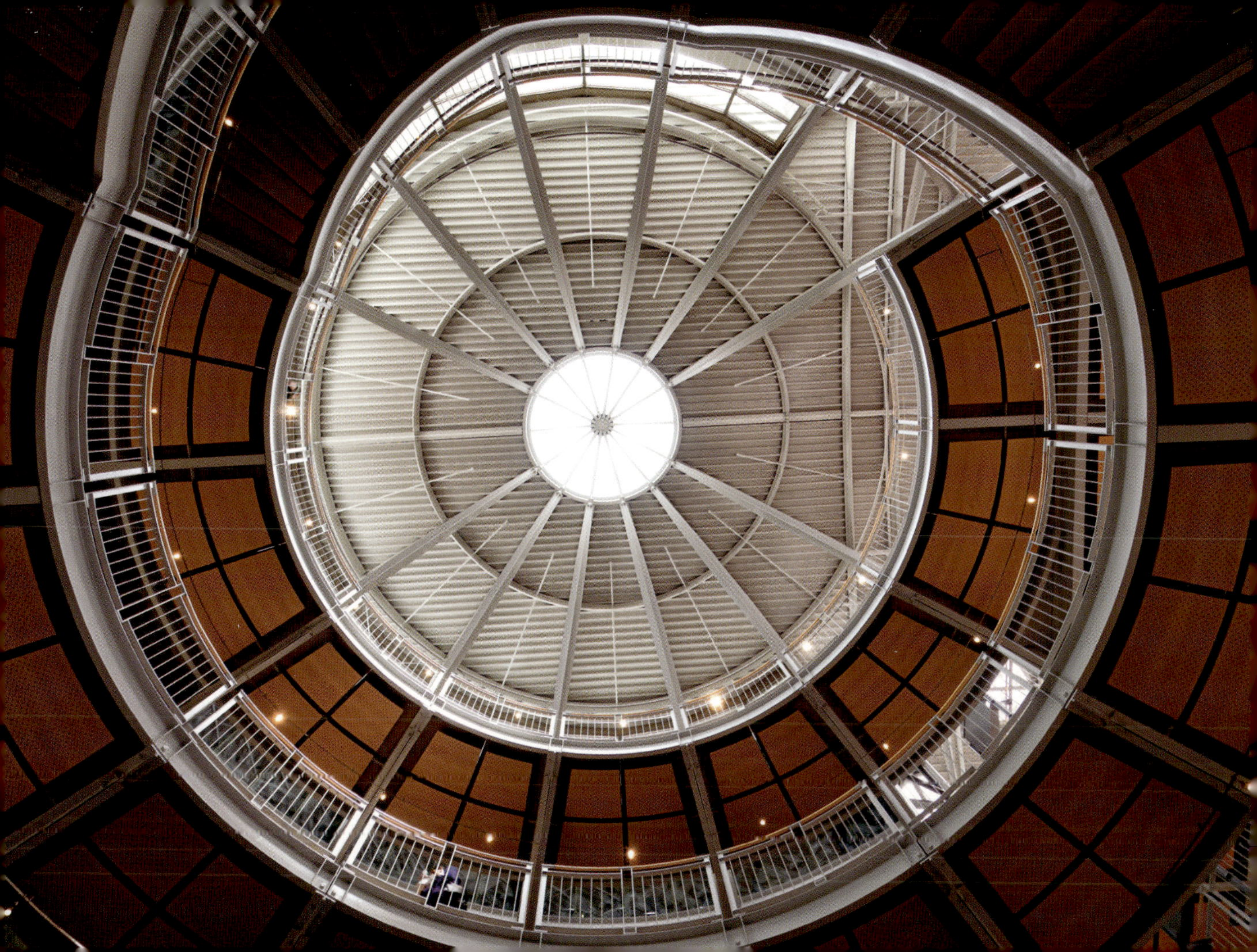

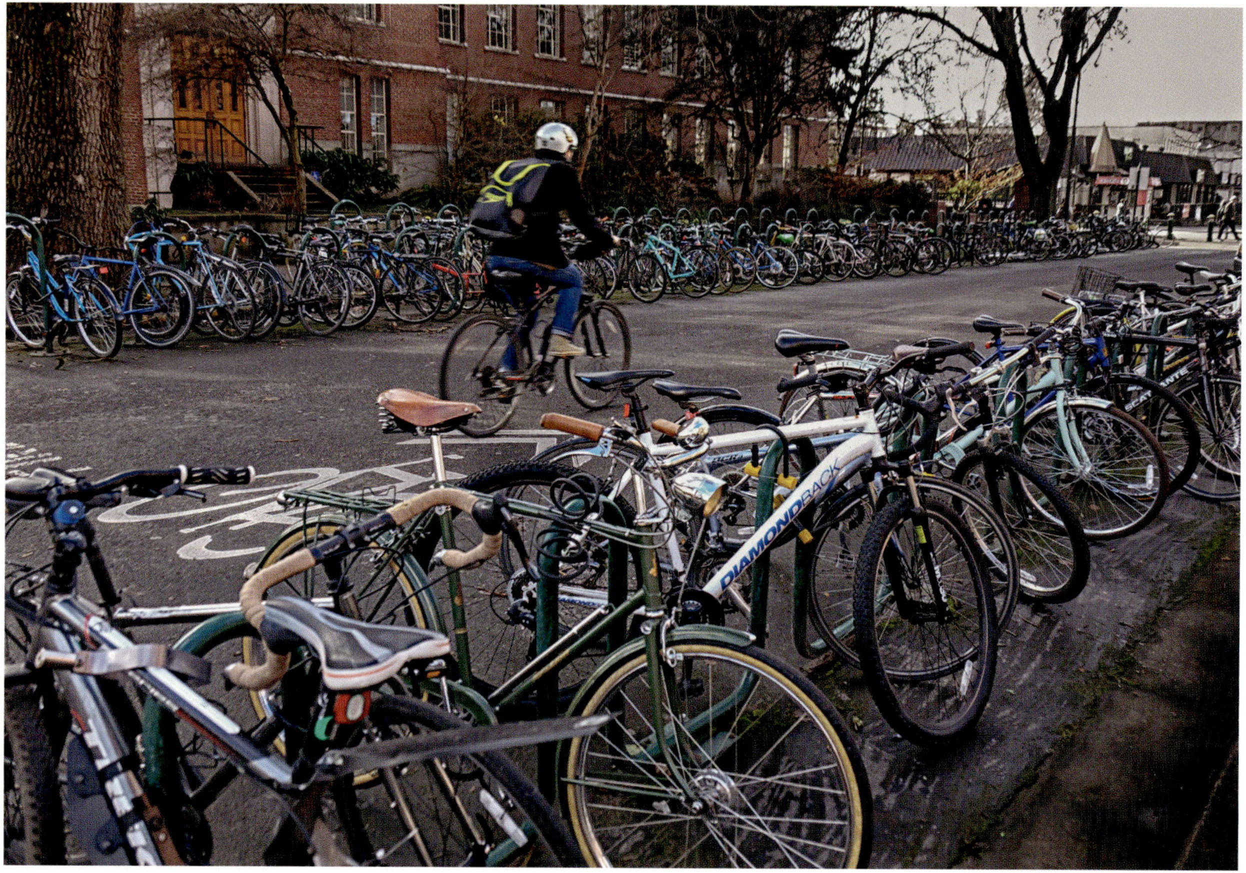
DIAMONDBACK

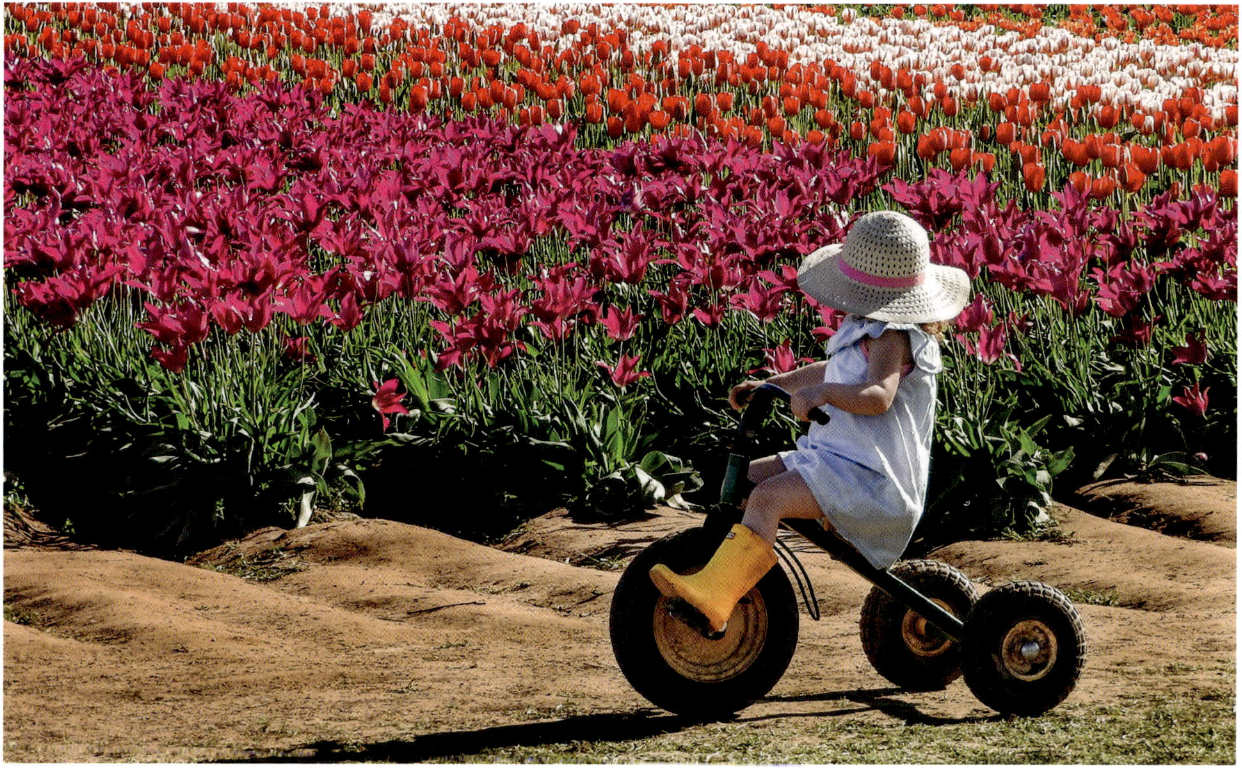

Bicycles. University of Oregon, Eugene.
Photo by Barbara Tricarico

Wooden Shoe Tulip Farm, Woodburn.
Photo by Charles Hillestad

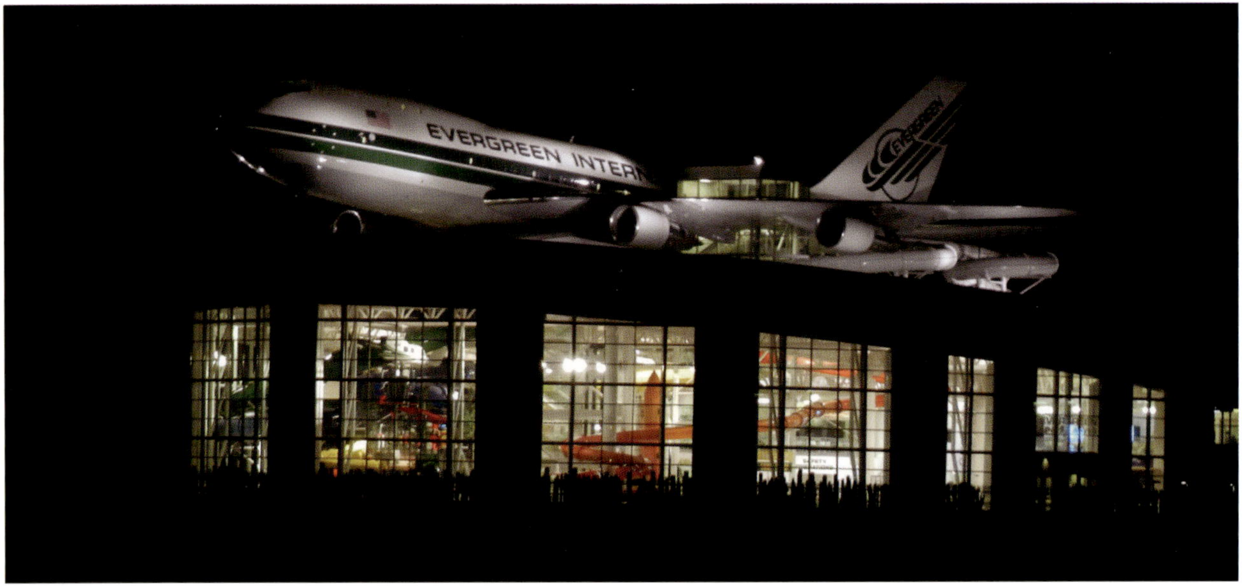

Evergreen Aviation & Space Museum's indoor Wings & Waves Waterpark, just outside McMinnville. *Photo by Charles Hillestad*

"Spruce Goose" at Evergreen Aviation Museum, outside McMinnville. The museum was built expressly to house Howard Hughes's gigantic birch airplane, flown only once during World War II. It is the largest wooden airplane ever constructed. *Photo by Charles Hillestad*

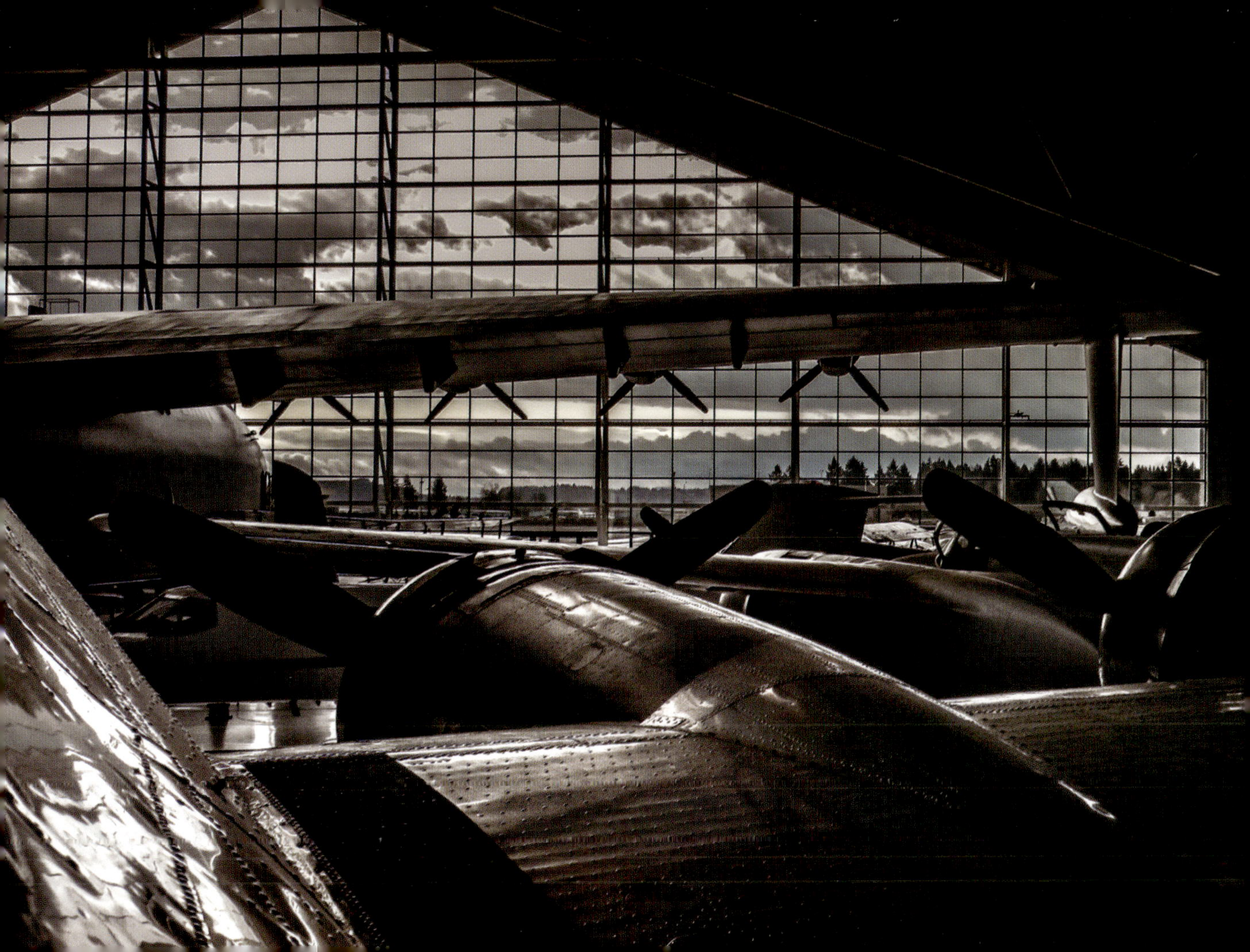

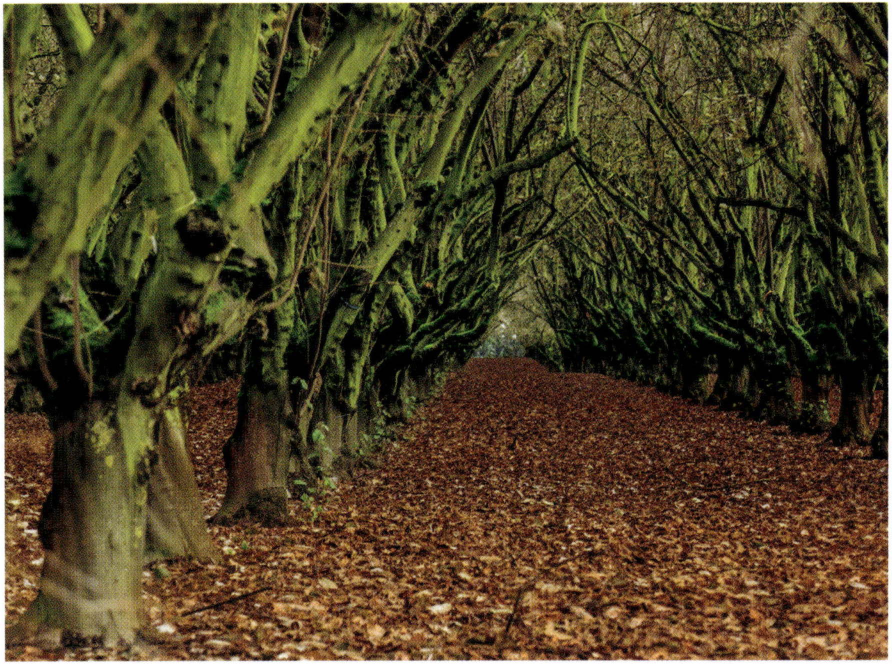

Hazelnut farm, Willamette Valley. *Photo by Vivian McAleavey*

Abacela Winery, Roseburg. *Photo by Vivian McAleavey*

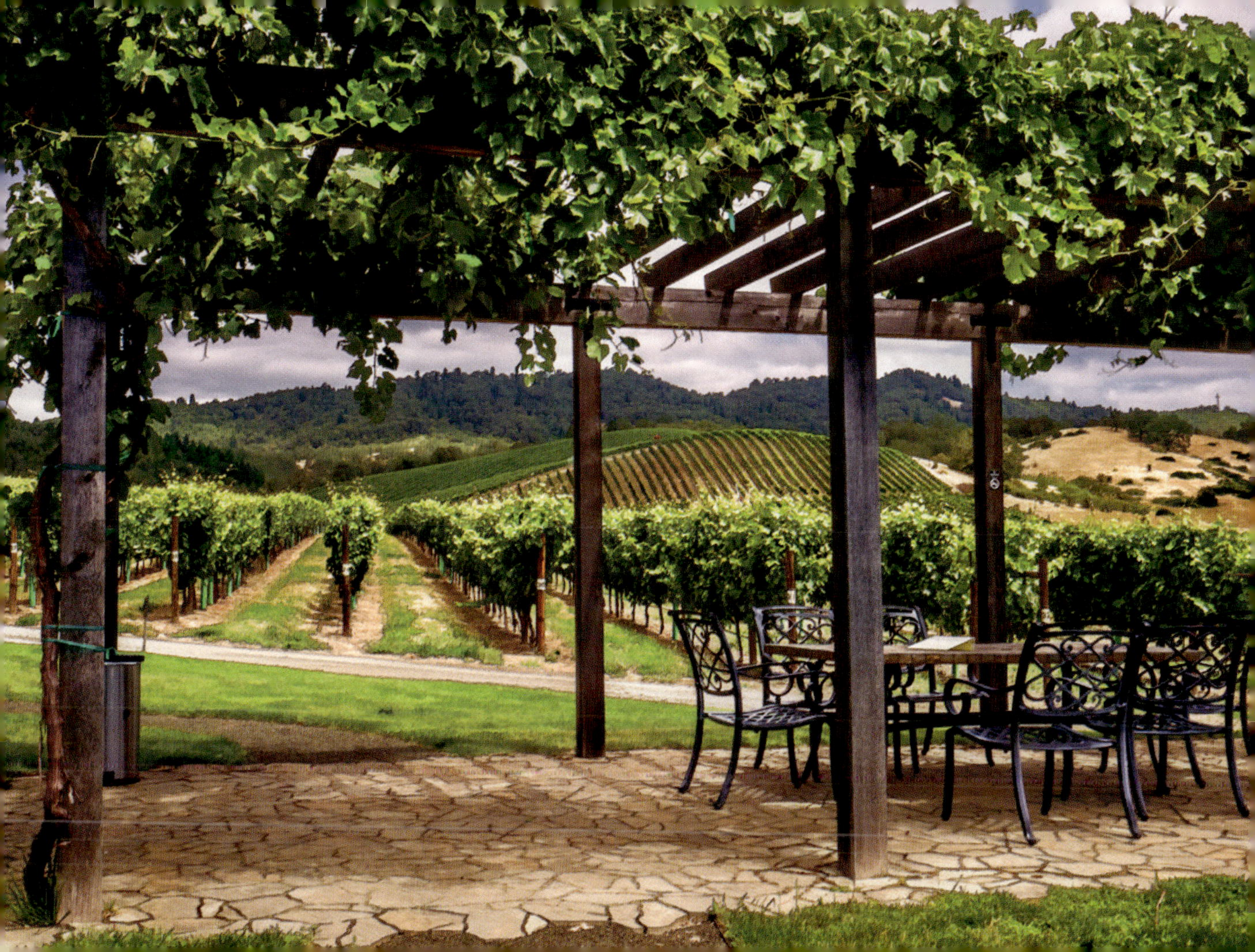

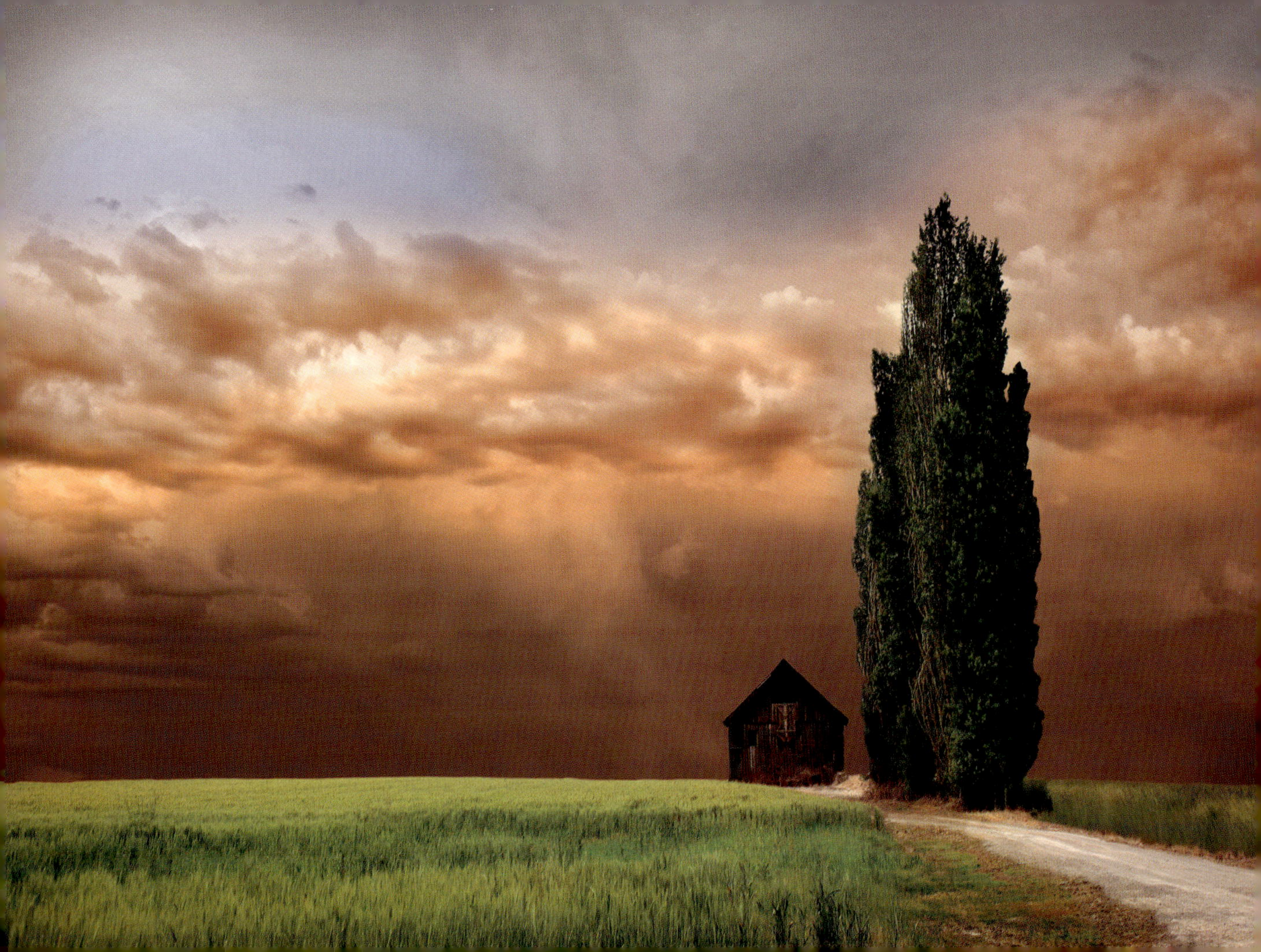

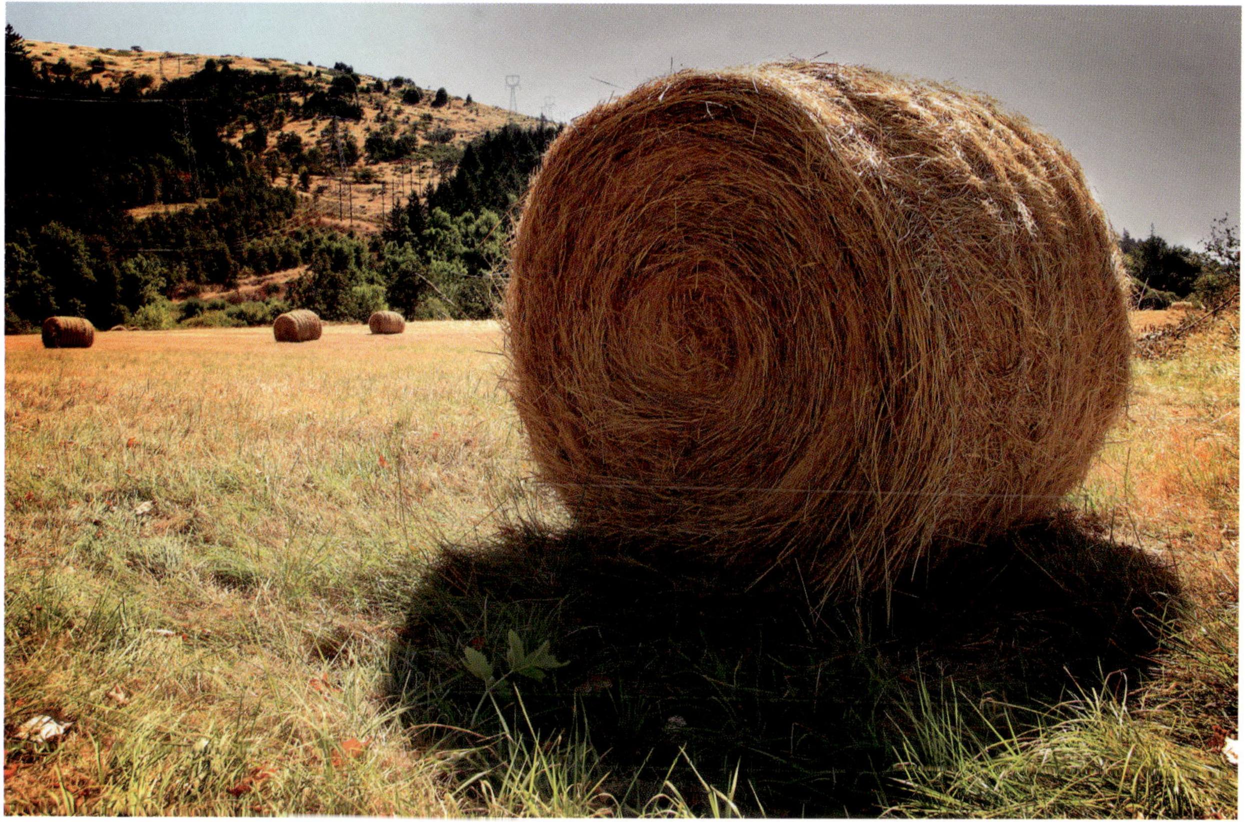

Farm country. *Photo by John Kirk*

Hay bales. *Photo by John Kirk*

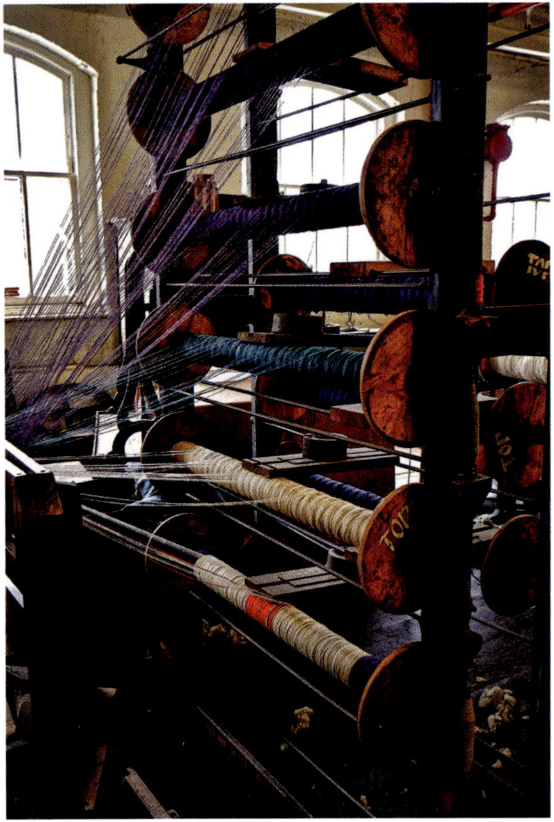

Thomas Kay Woolen Mill interior, Willamette Heritage Center, Salem. *Photo by Richard Krieger*

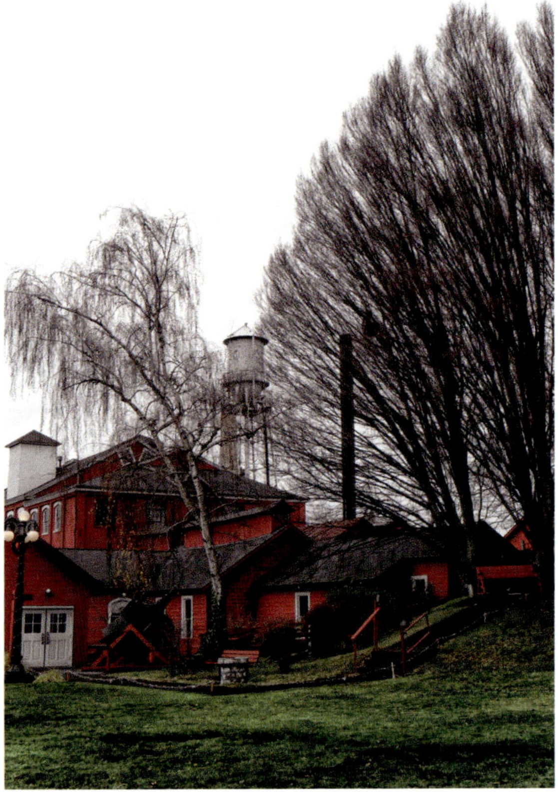

Thomas Kay Woolen Mill buildings at the Willamette Heritage Center, Salem. *Photo by Richard Krieger*

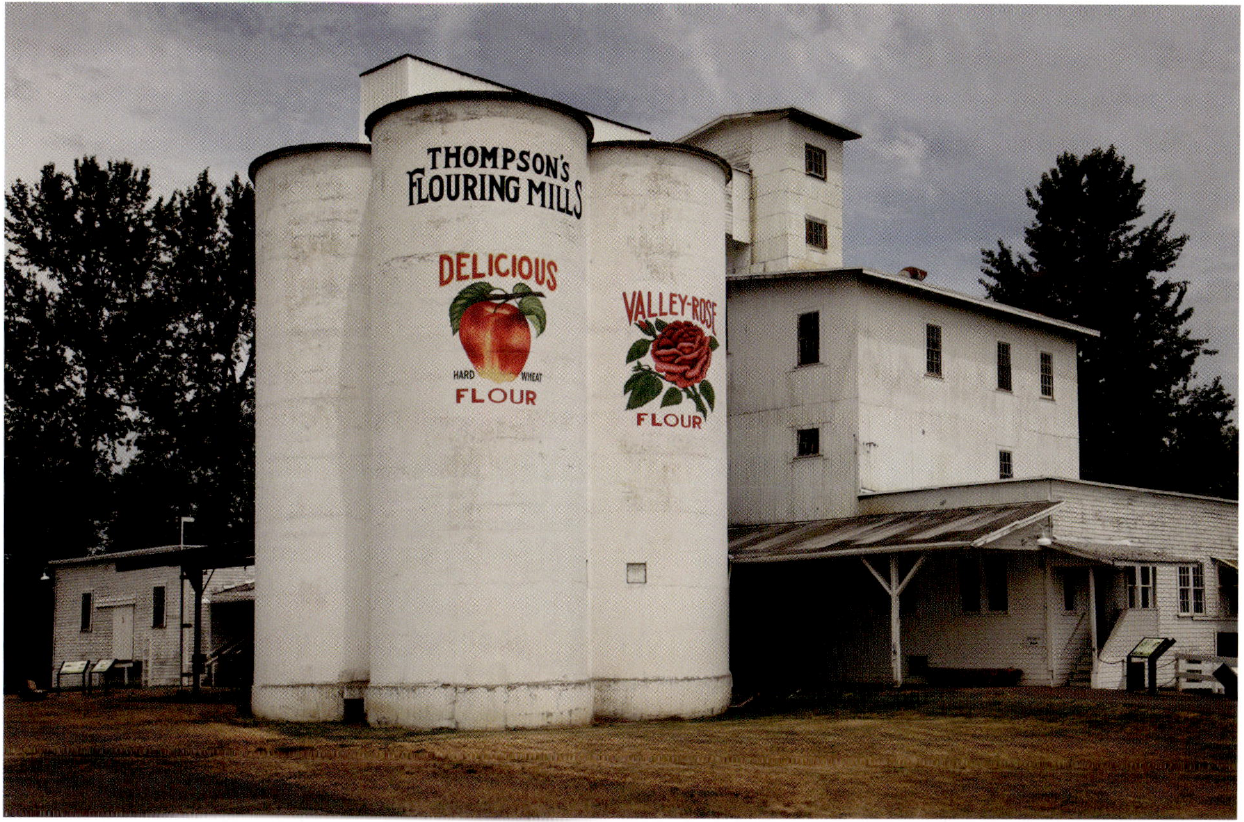

Thompson's Mills State Heritage Site, the oldest existing waterpowered grain mill in the state, Shedd. *Photo by John Kirk*

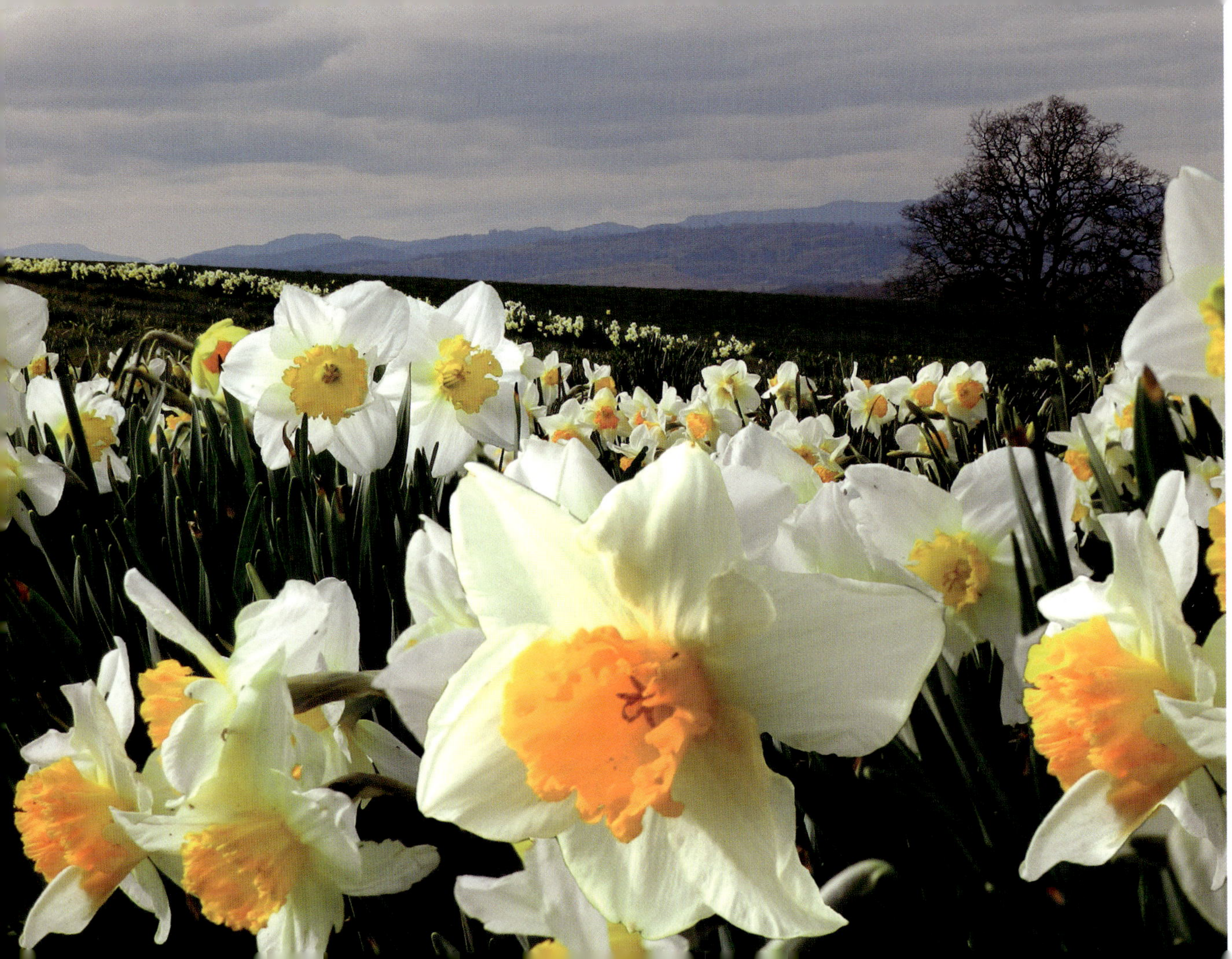

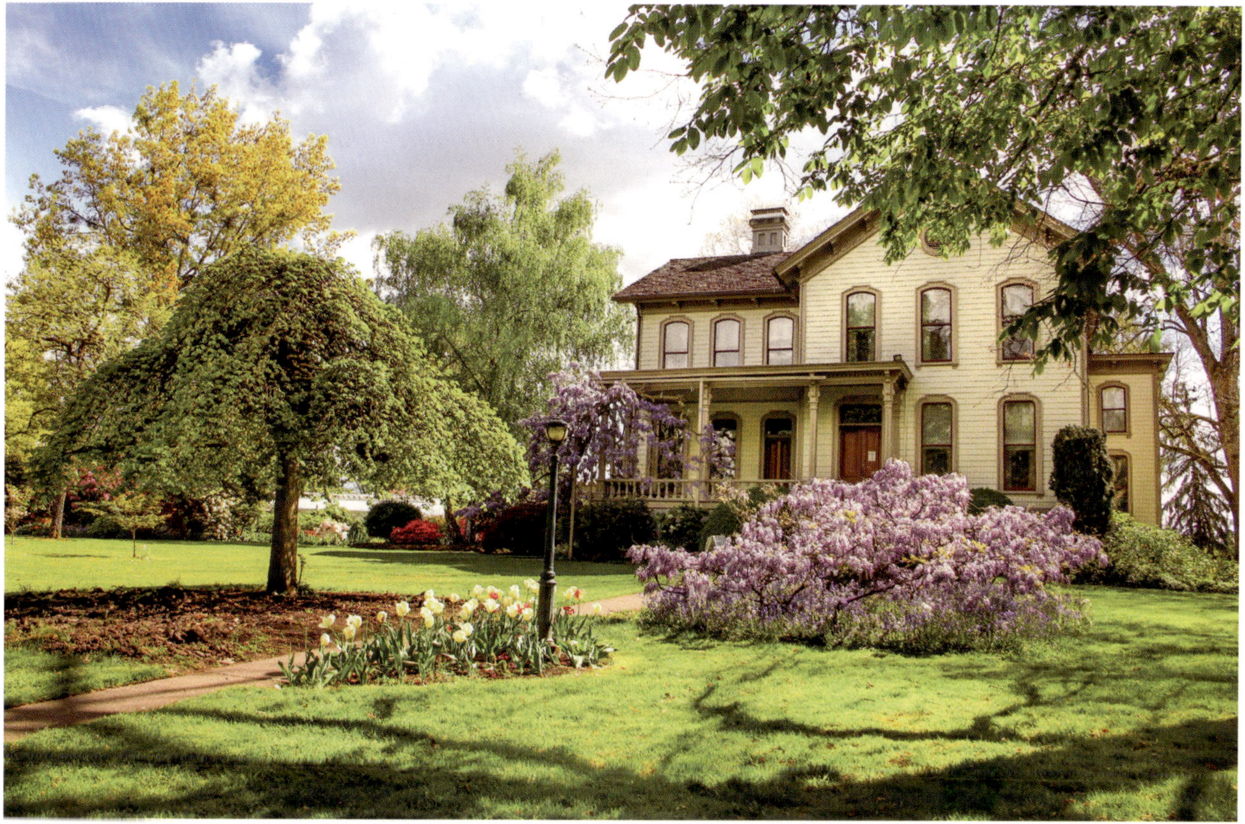

Commercial fields of daffodils near Amity. *Photo by Charles Hillestad*

Bush Park Museum, Salem. In 1877, this Victorian house was built for Asahel Bush, founder of the *Oregon Statesman* newspaper. *Photo by Terry Fisher*

32

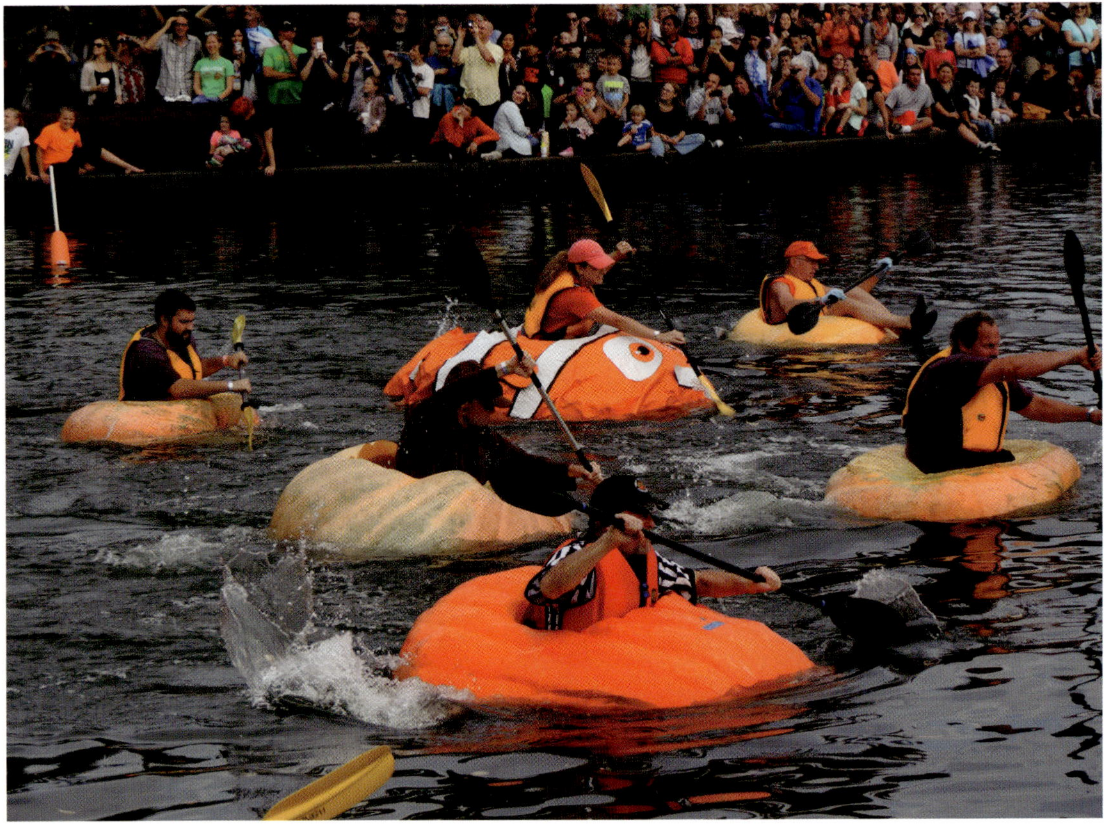

Pumpkin Regatta in Tualatin. *Photo by Charles Hillestad*

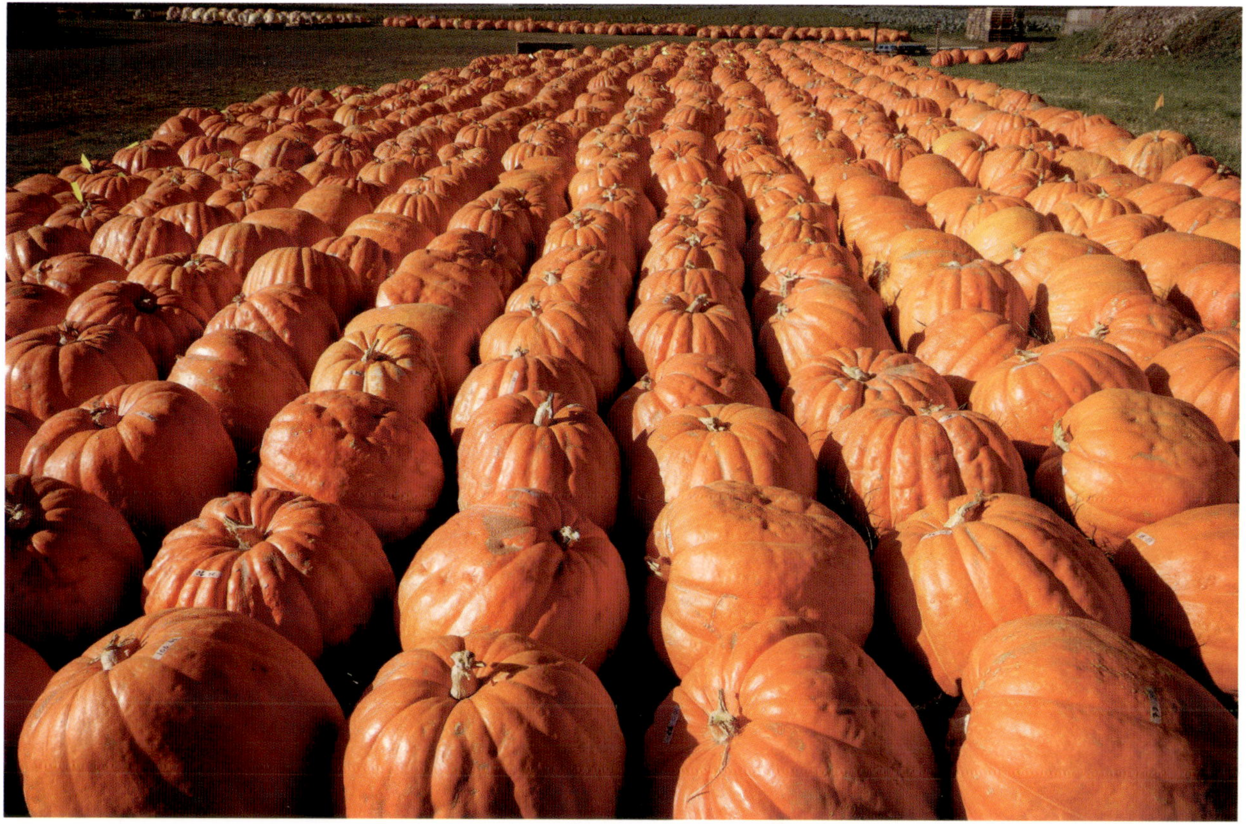

Pumpkins, Willamette Valley. *Photo by John Kirk*

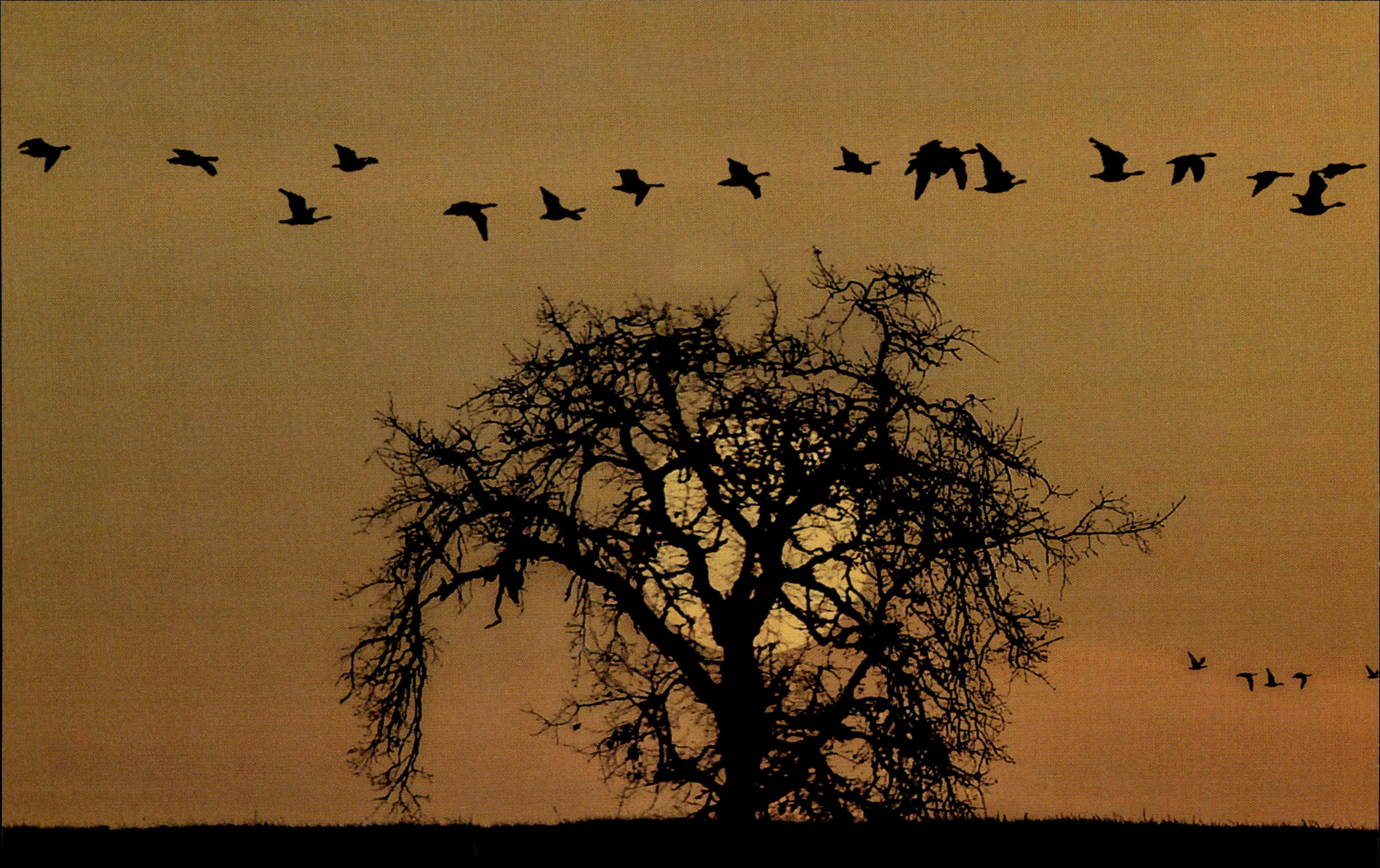

36

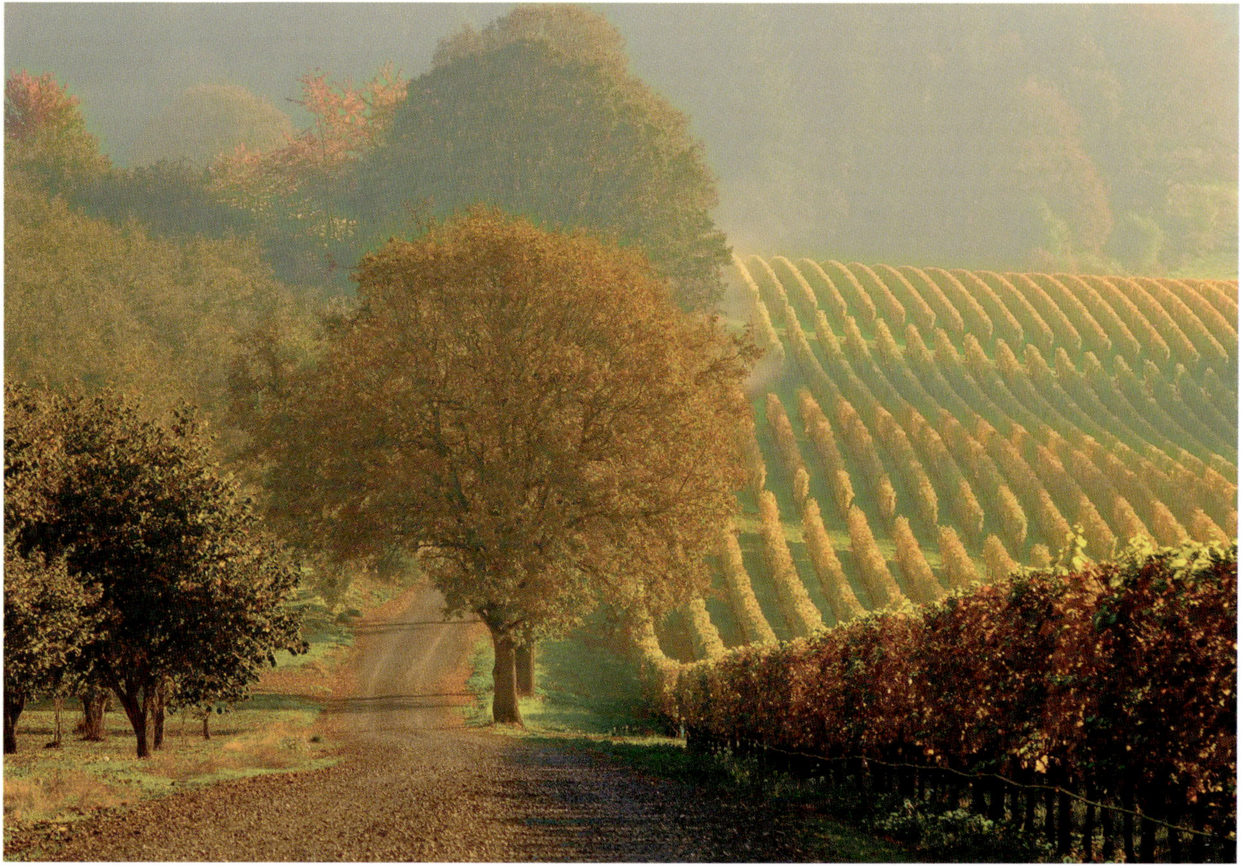

Autumn in the Dundee Hills Vineyards.
Photo by Clem Paslack

Forest Grove Sidewalk Chalk Festival.
Photo by Charles Hillestad

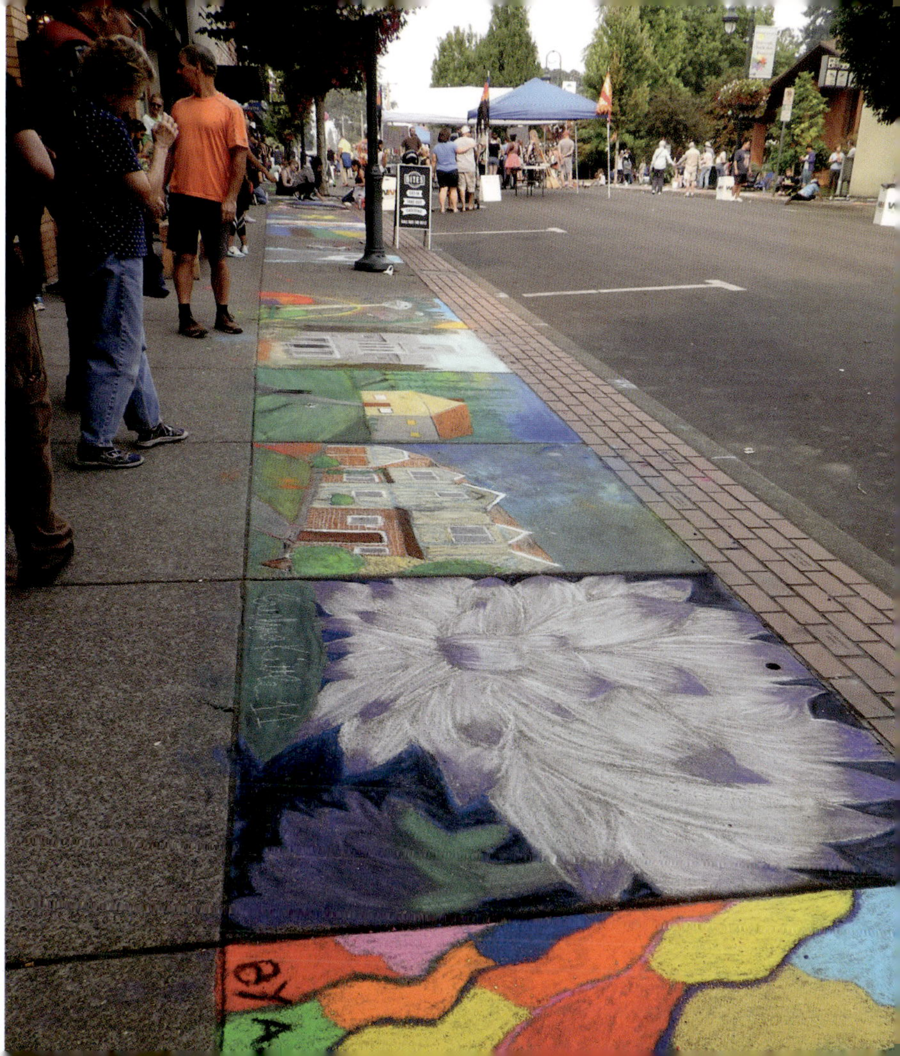

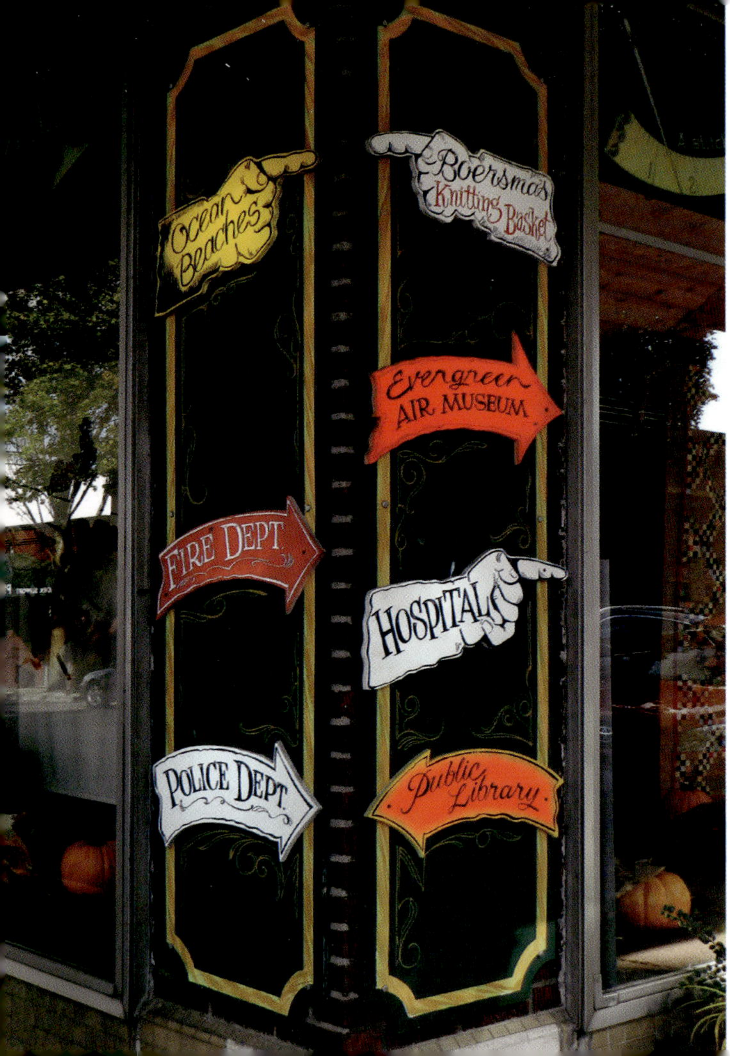

McMinnville directional signs.
Photo by Charles Hillestad

McMinnville farmers' market.
Photo by Charles Hillestad

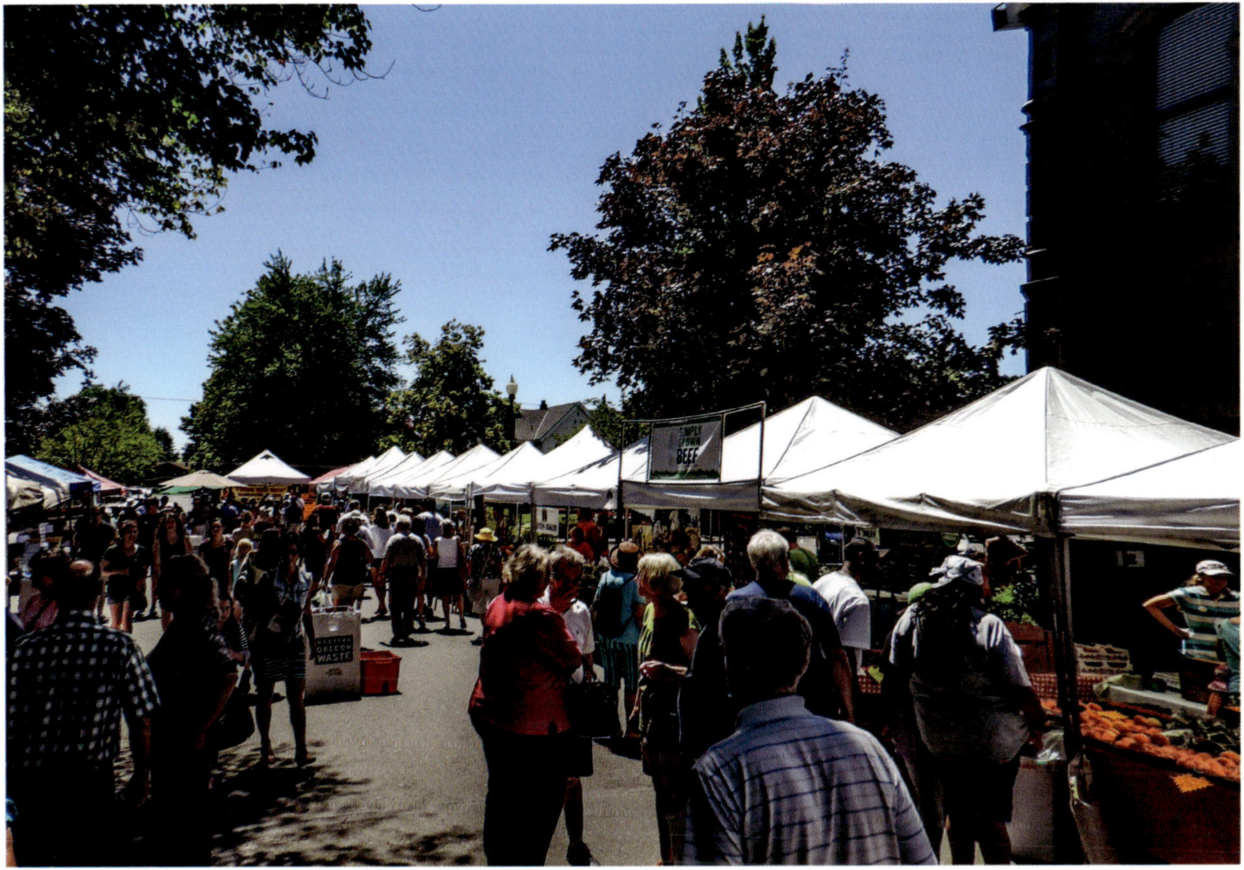
BEEF
WASTE

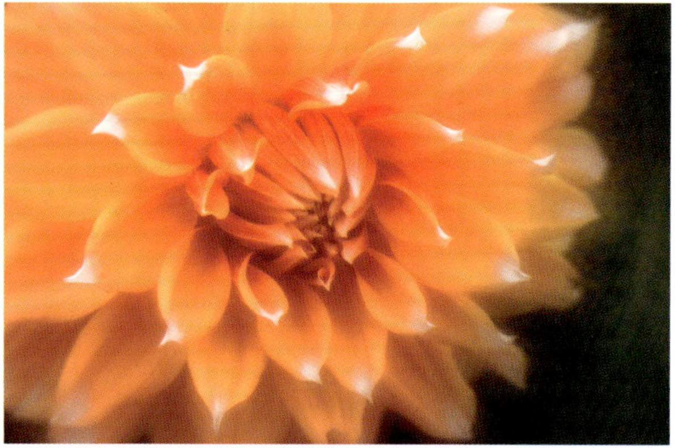

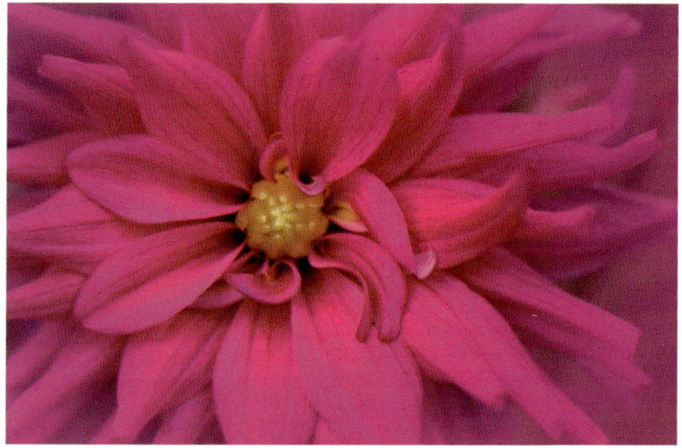

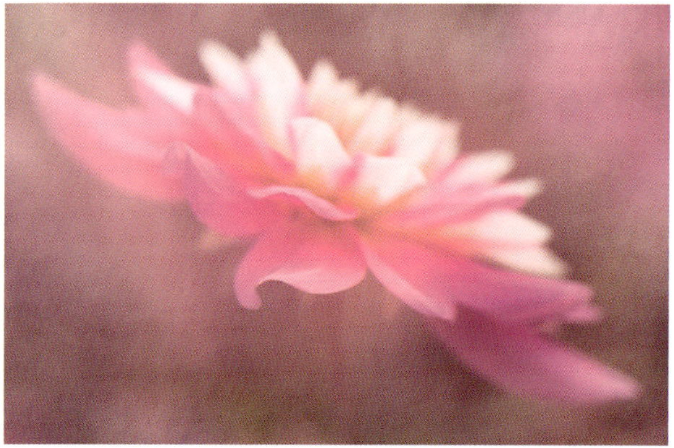

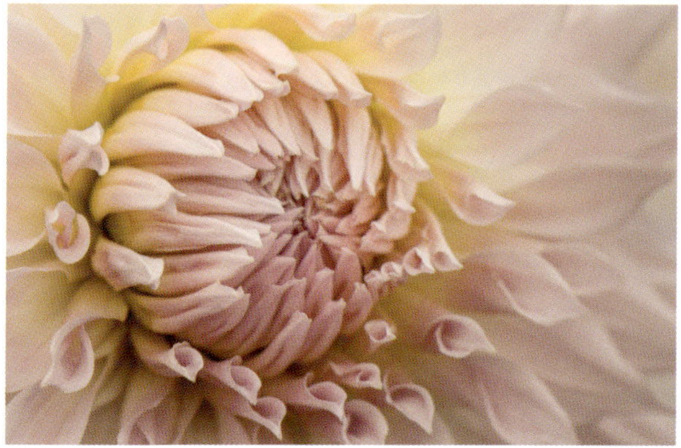

"Creamsicle," Swan Island Dahlia Festival, Canby. *Photo by Julie Bonney*

"Gingham Girl," Swan Island Dahlia Festival, Canby. *Photo by Julie Bonney*

Oregon Gardens dahlia. *Photo by Julie Bonney*

"KA's Cloud," Swan Island Dahlia Festival, Canby. *Photo by Julie Bonney*

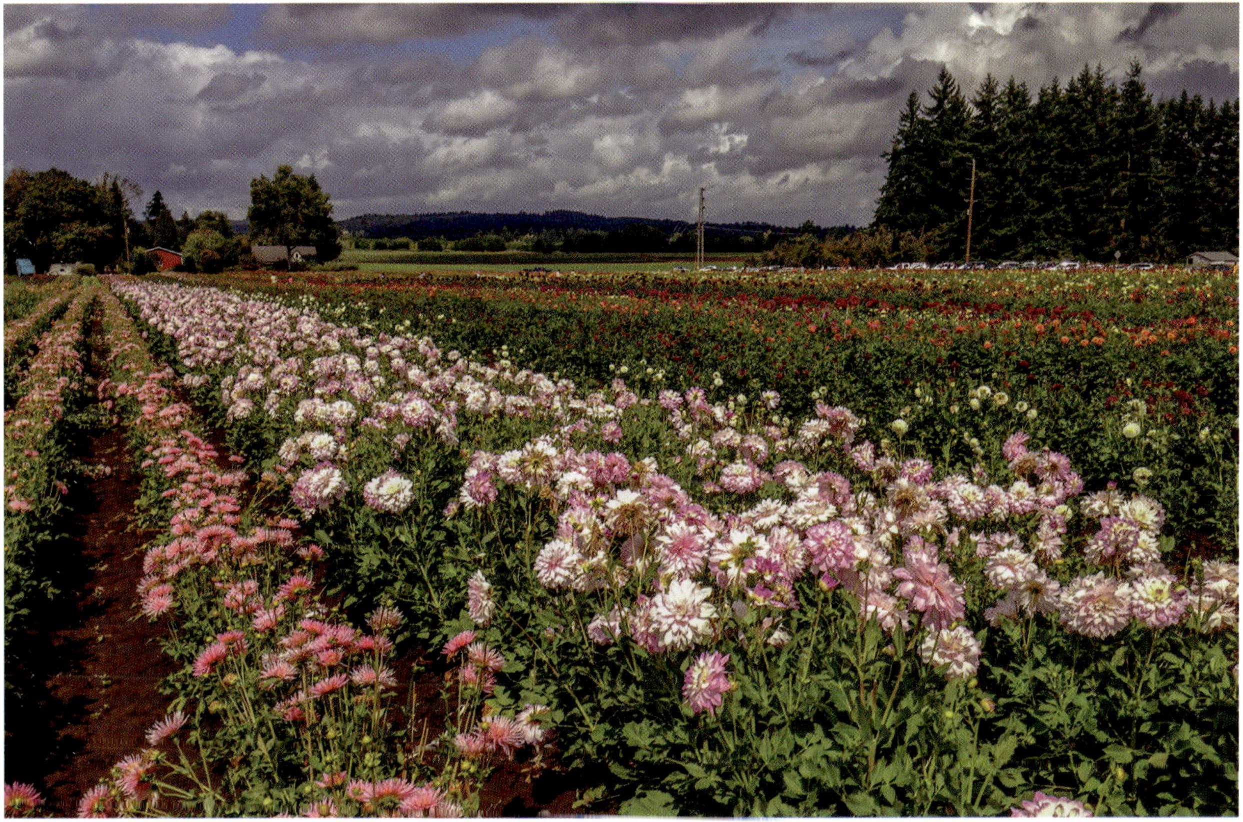

Swan Island dahlias, Canby. *Photo by Alana Lynn Starkweather*

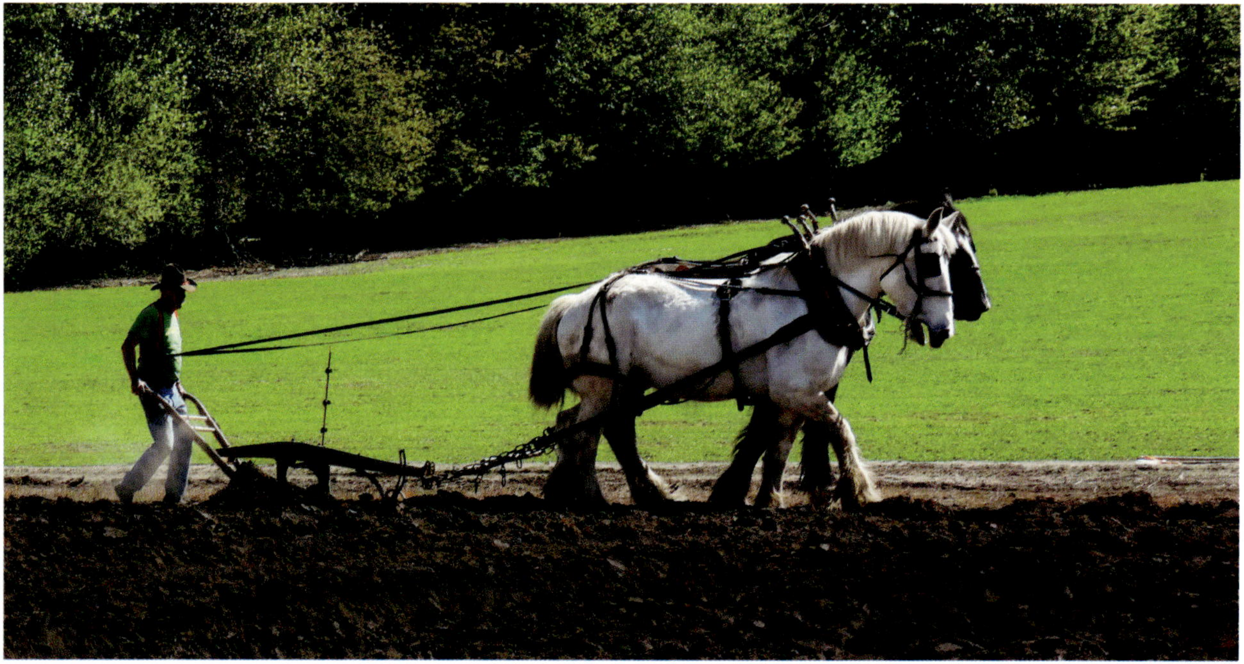

Plowing competition at Yamhill Valley Heritage Center's Farm Festival.
Photo by Charles Hillestad

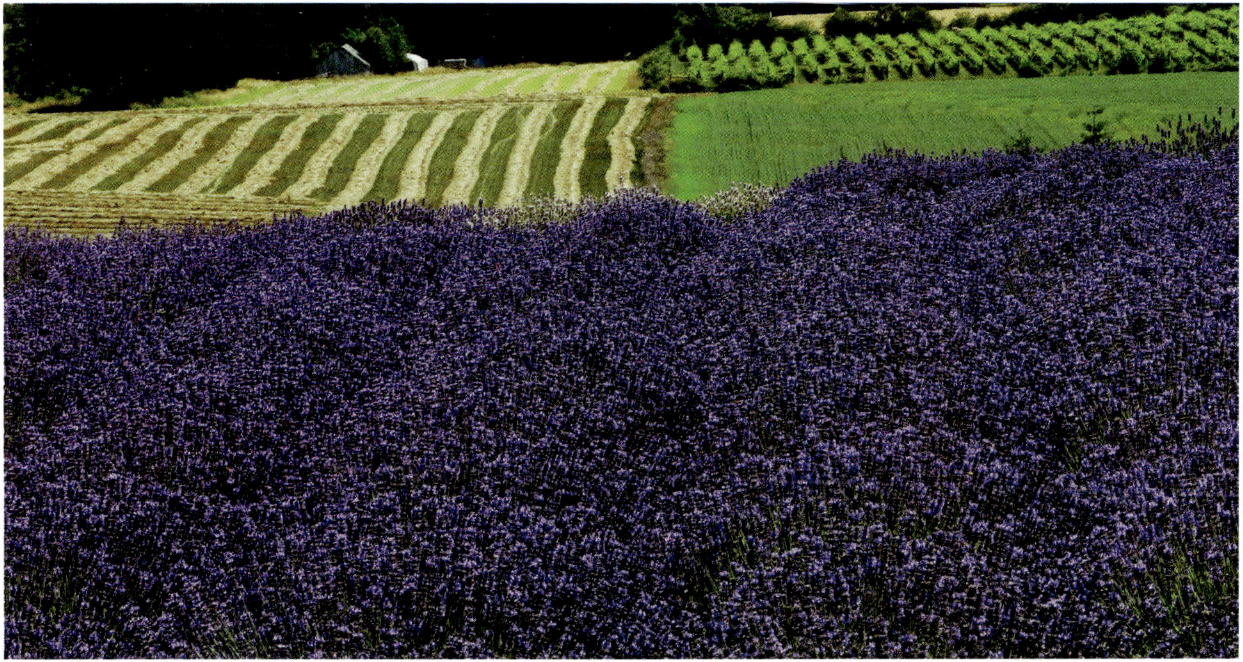

Annual lavender festival near Carlton.
Photo by Charles Hillestad

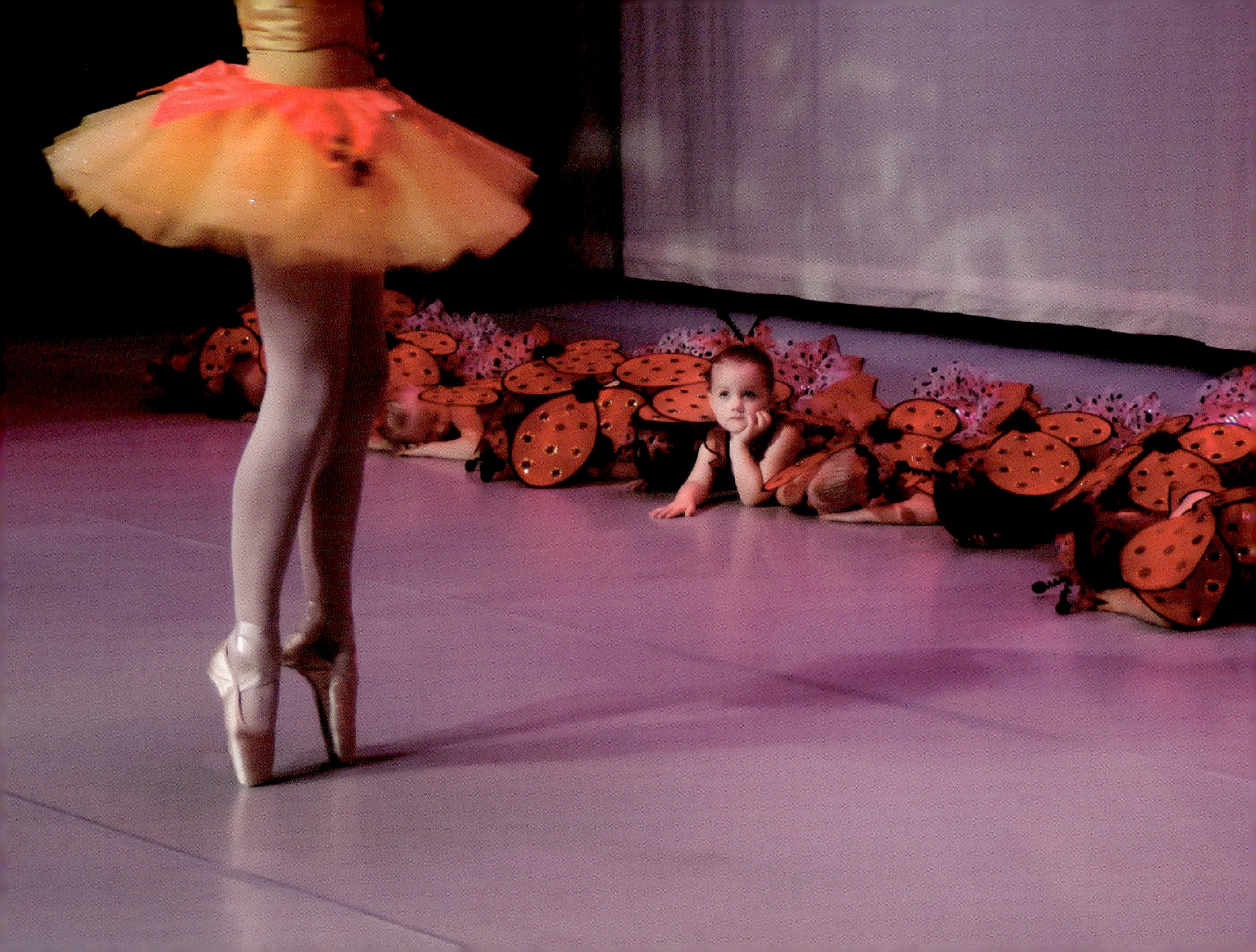

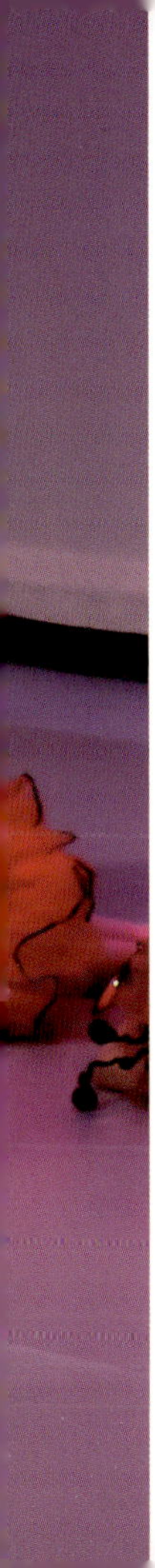

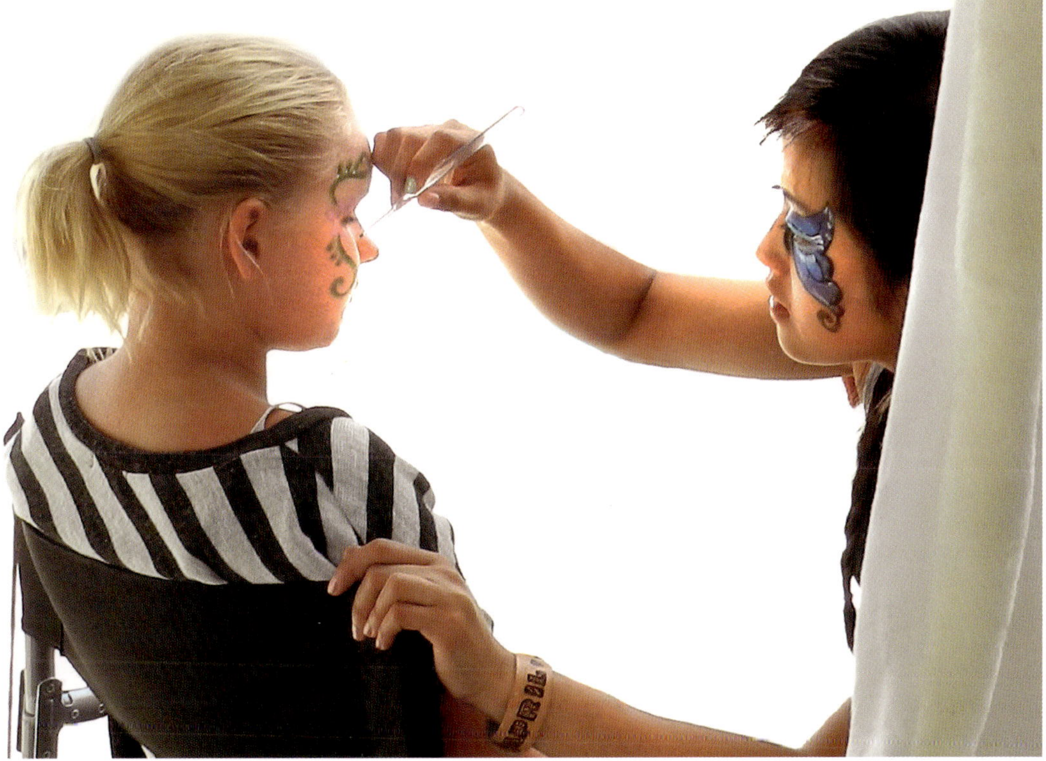

Performance by aspiring dancers at Gallery Ballet & Tap School in McMinnville. *Photo by Charles Hillestad*

Face painting at TurkeyRama, McMinnville. The TurkeyRama Festival has been in existence for over fifty years. *Photo by Charles Hillestad*

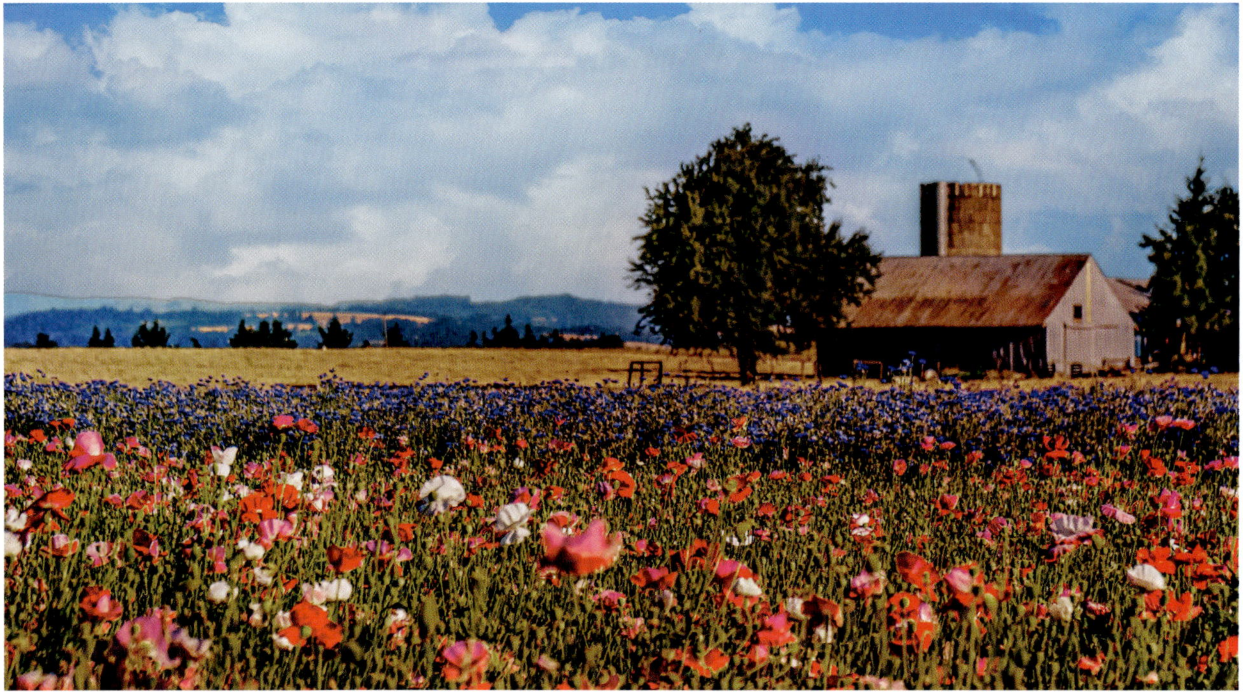

Flower field near Mt. Angel. *Photo by Cornelius Matteo*

Annual dahlia festival near Canby. *Photo by Charles Hillestad*

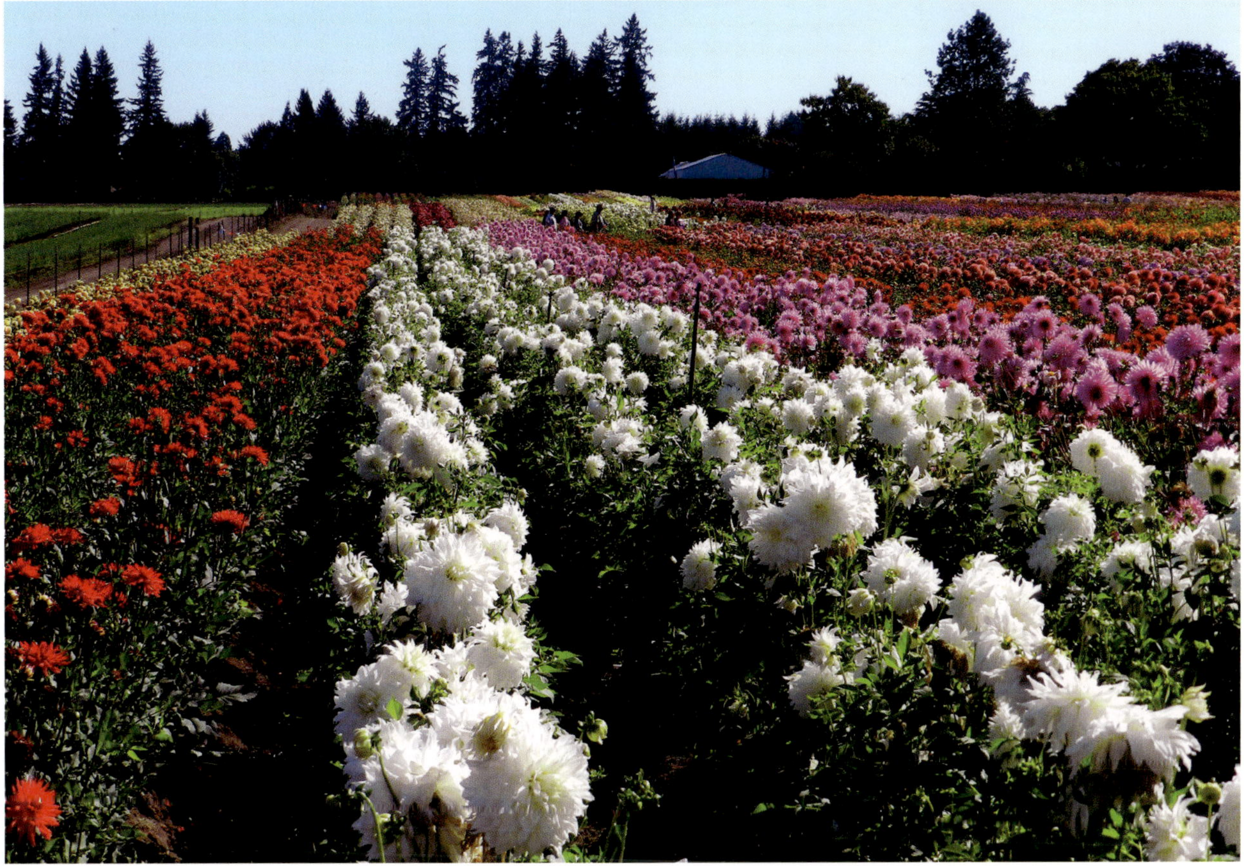

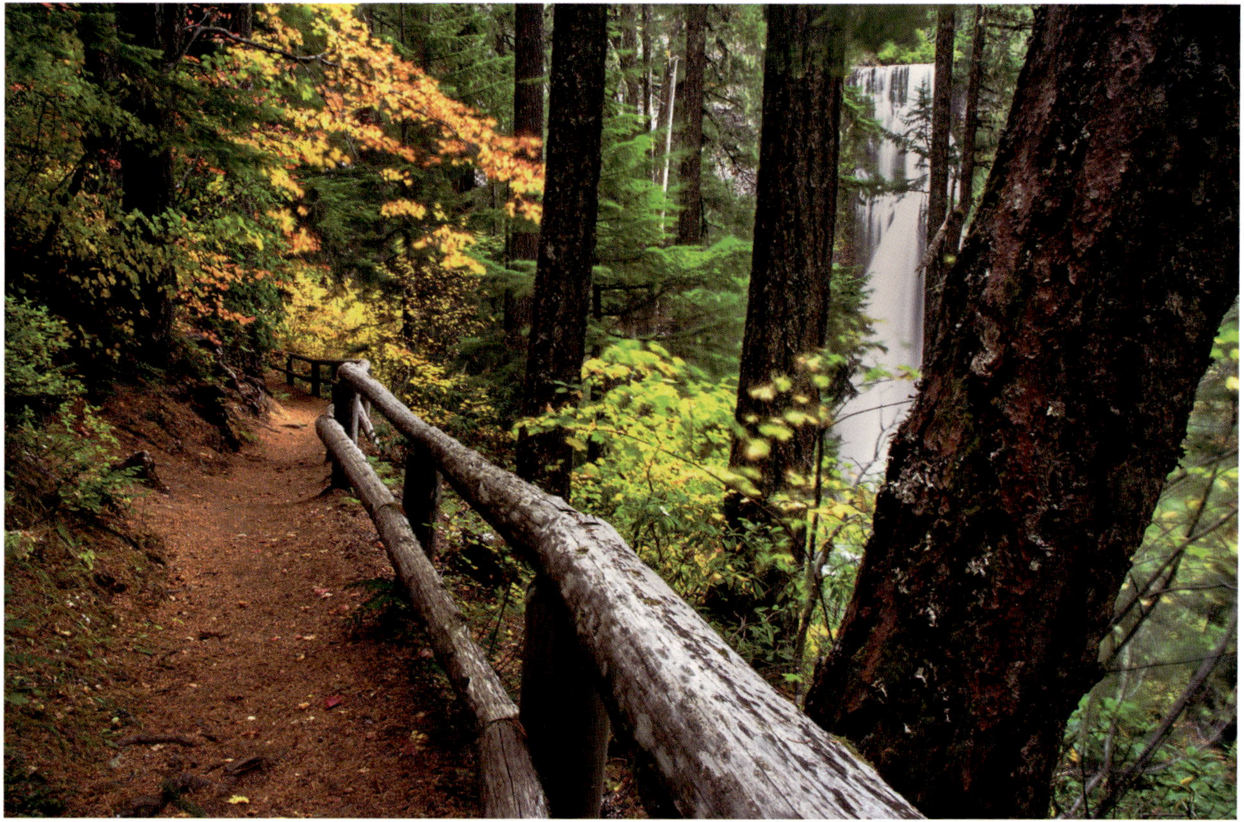

Salt Creek Falls Trail, Willamette National Forest.
Photo by Jay Newman

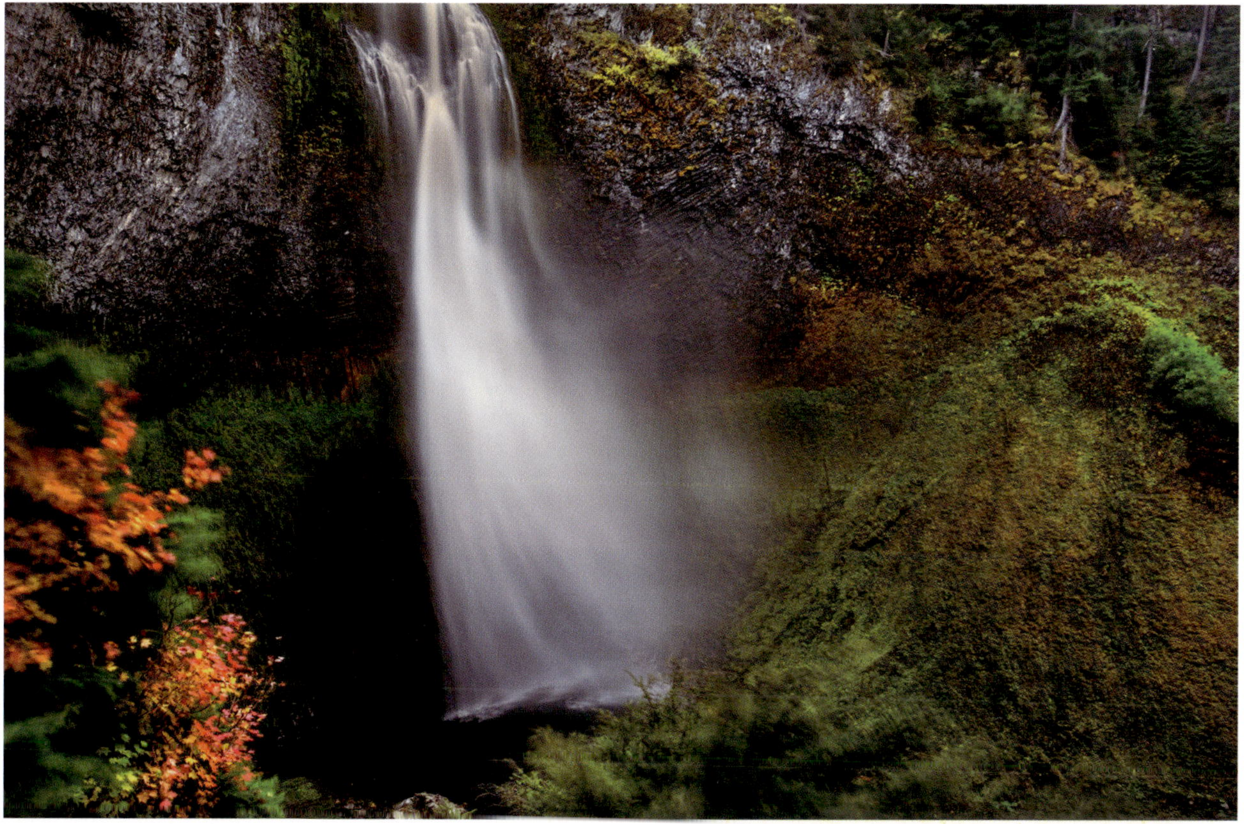

Salt Creek Falls, Willamette National Forest.
Photo by Sue Newman

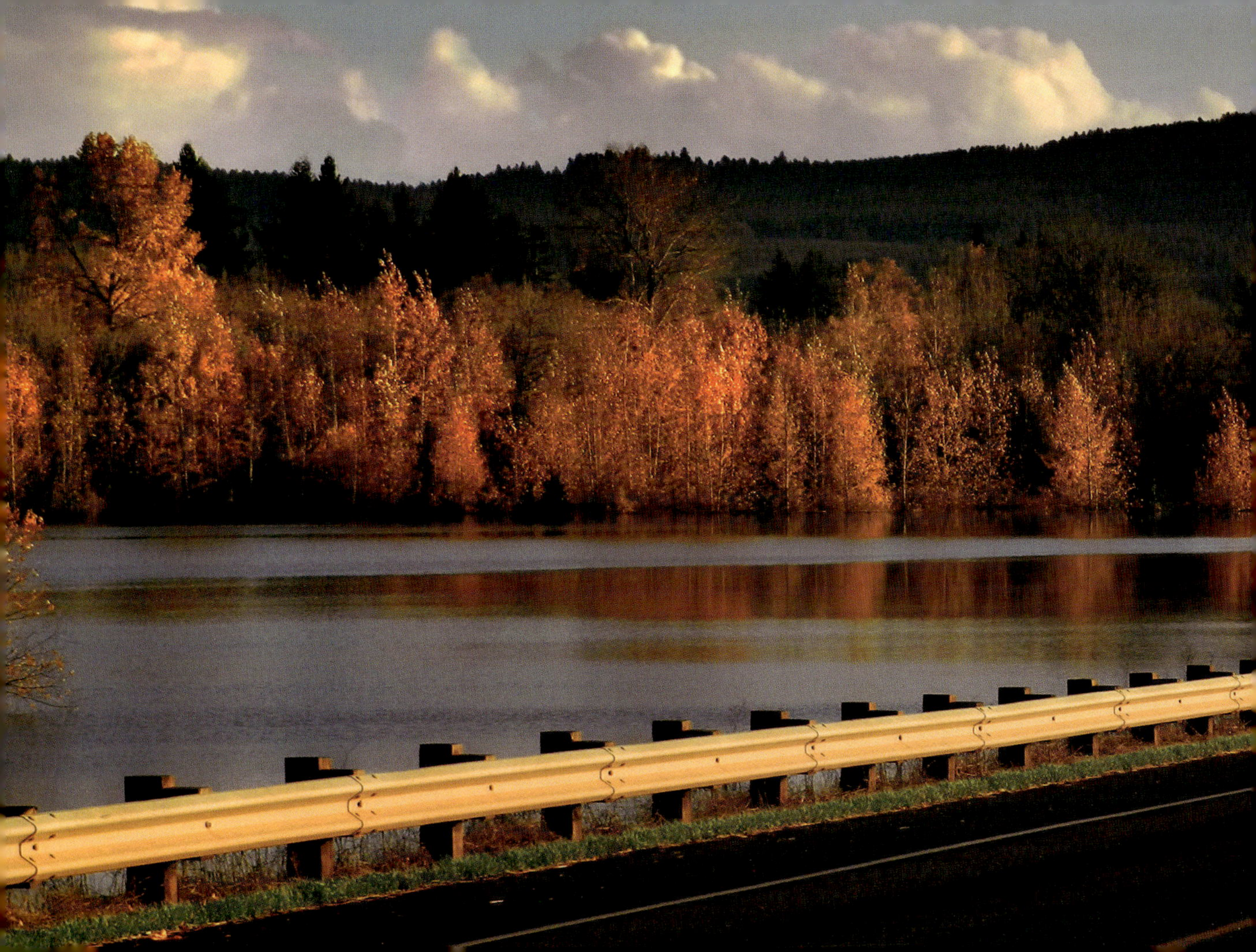

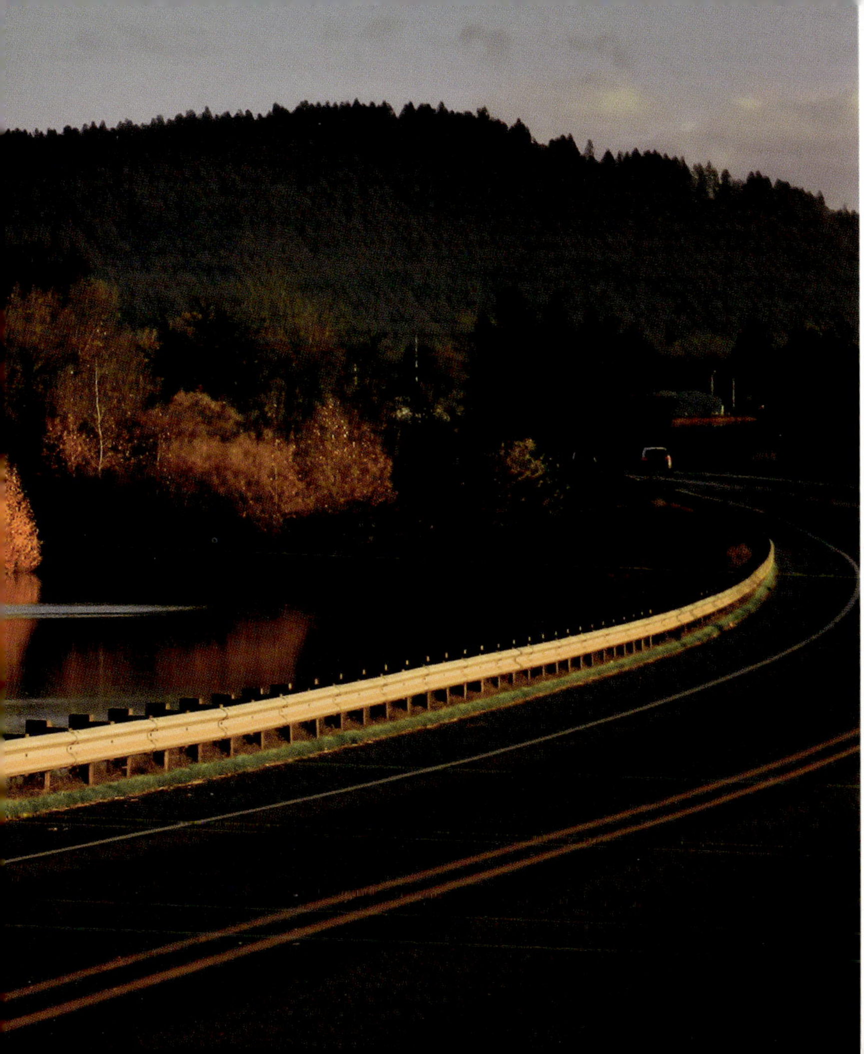

Highway 99 to Amity.
Photo by Charles Hillestad

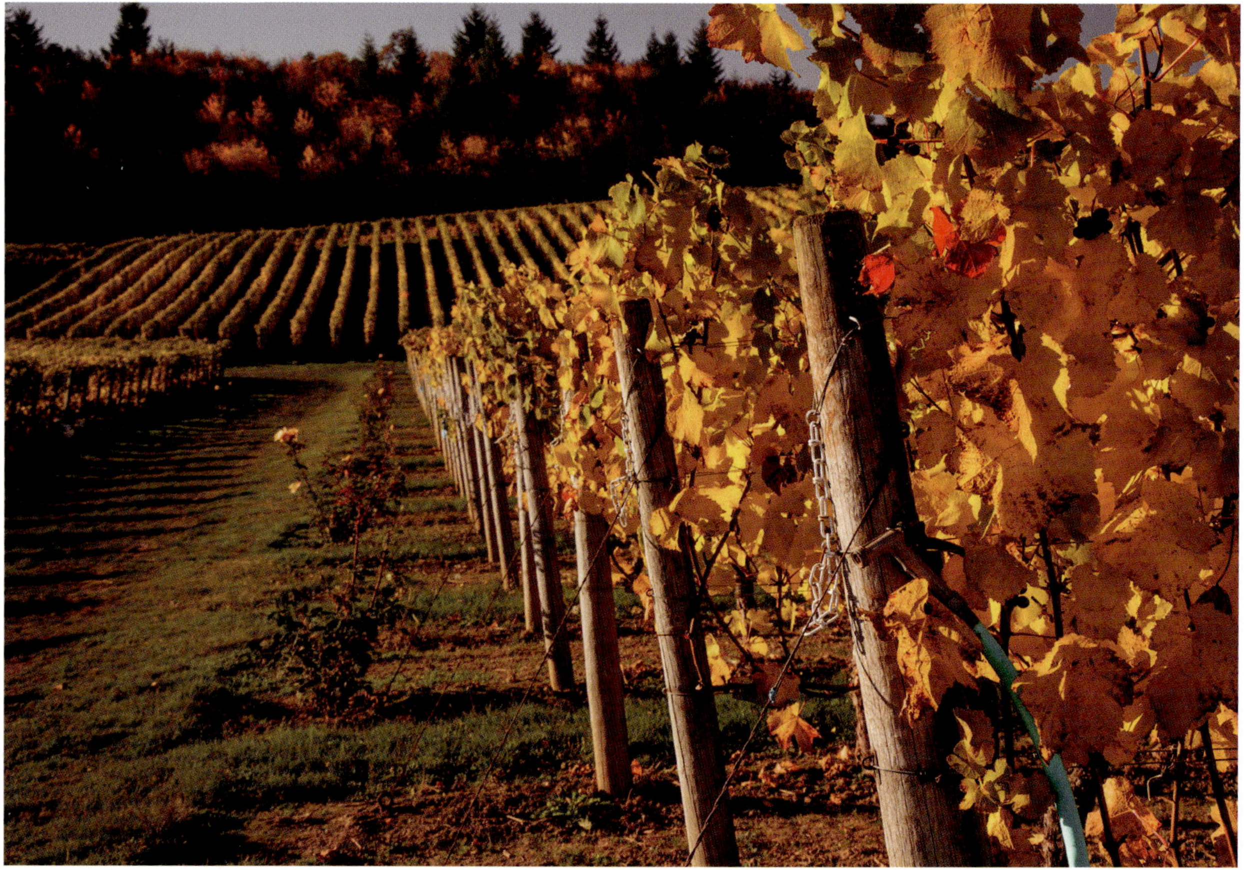

Fall in Willamette Valley Vineyards.
Photo by Kate Geary

South Falls. Visitors delight in walking behind the 177-foot waterfall. It is one of ten waterfalls in Silver Falls Park, the largest state park in Oregon.
Photo by Gary Hill

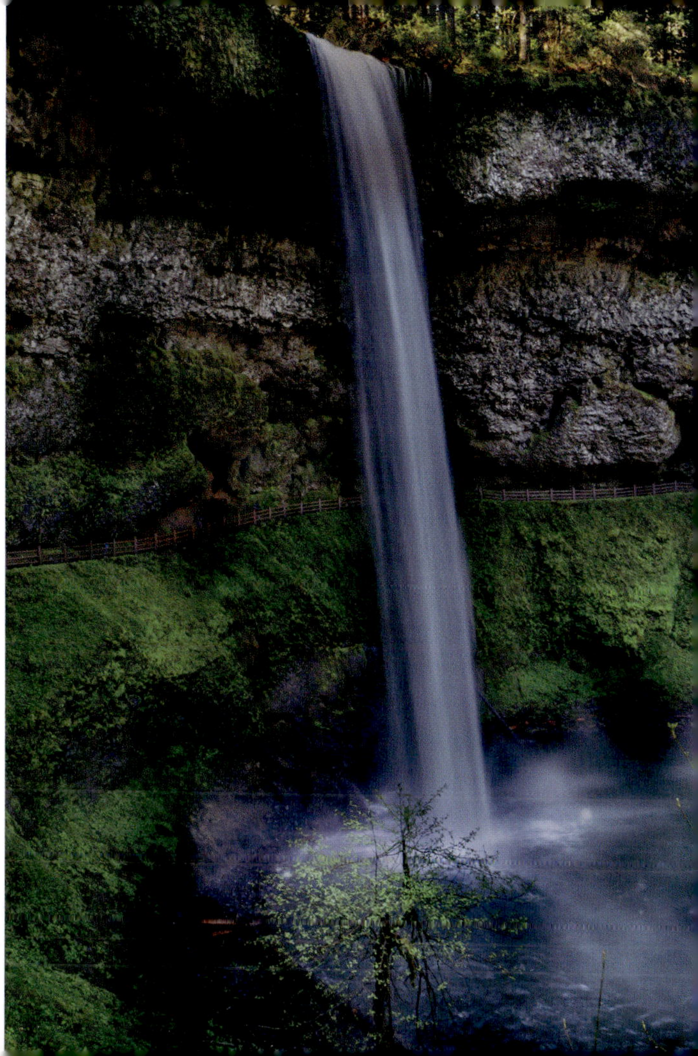

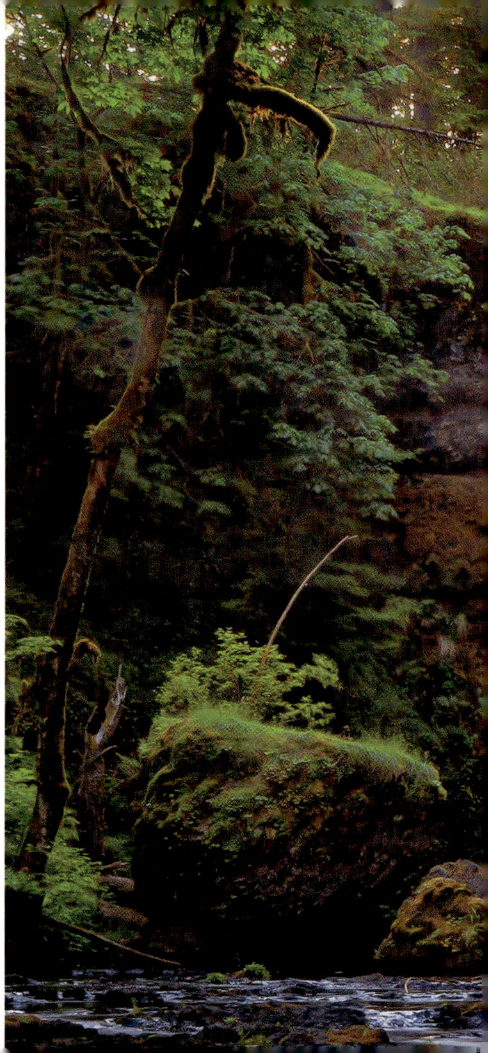

Upper North Falls, Silver Falls State Park.
Photo by John Christer Petersen

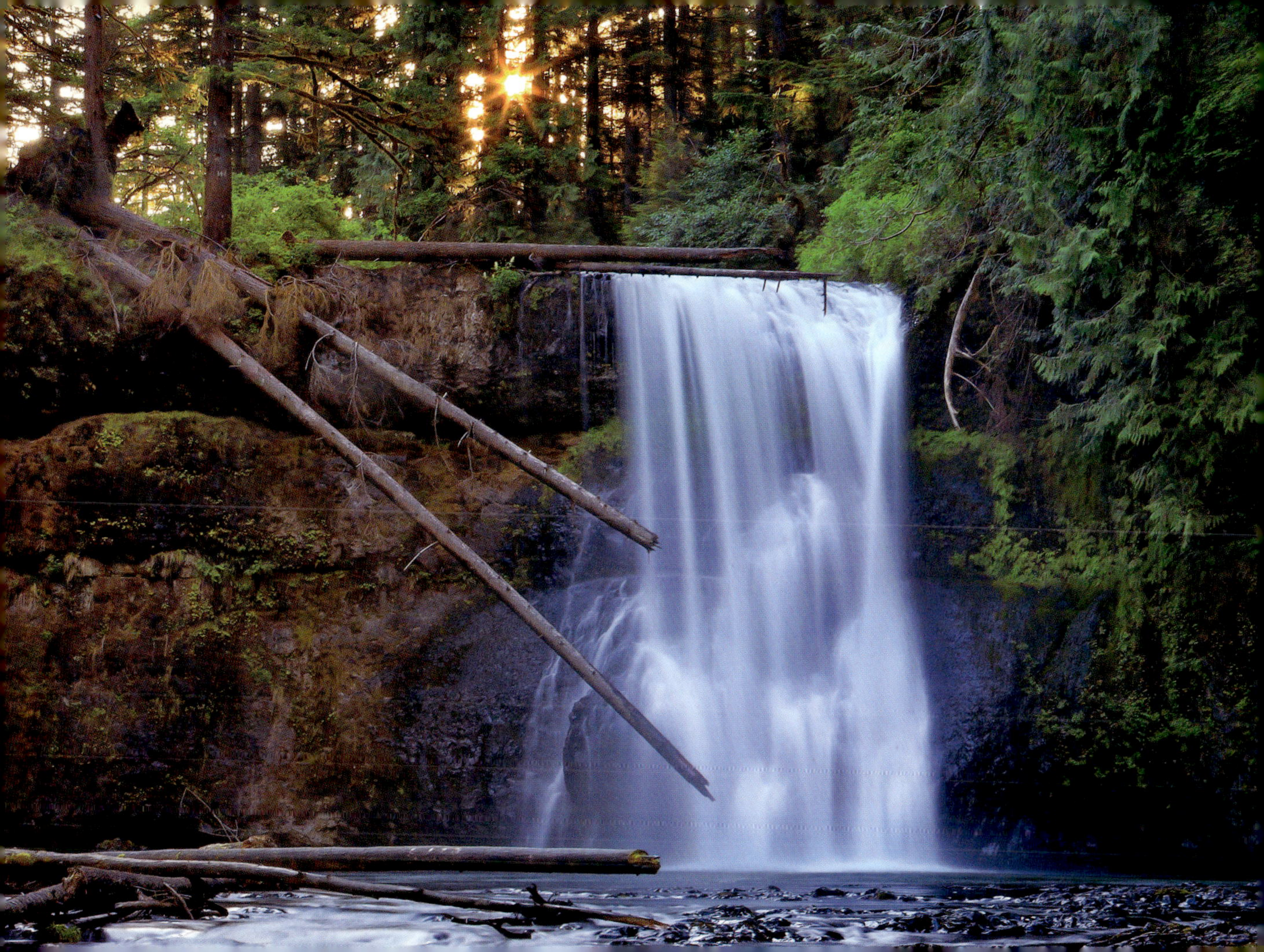

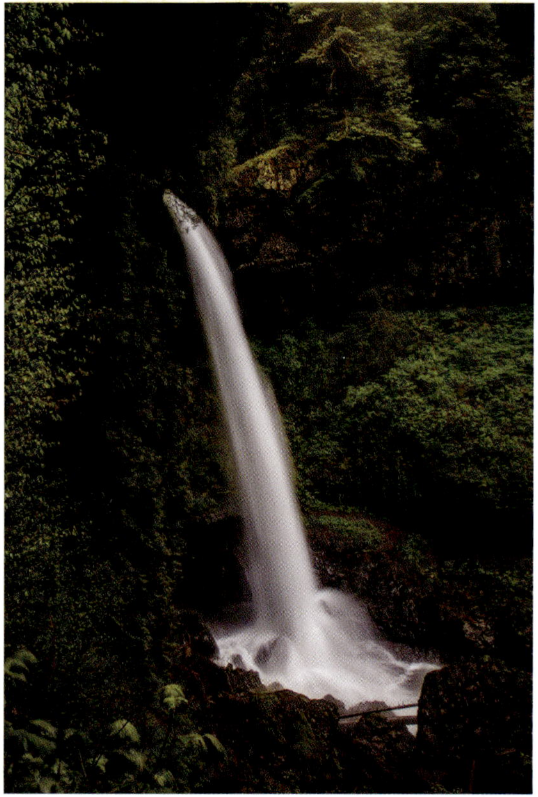

North Falls, at Silver Falls State Park. Silver Falls is often called the crown jewel of the Oregon State Parks system. *Photo by Alana Lynn Starkweather*

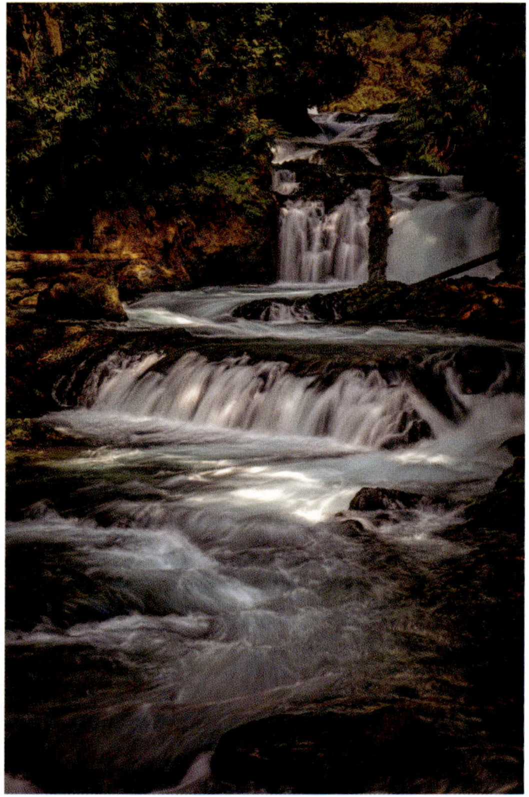

McKenzie River below Sahalie Falls. *Photo by Alana Lynn Starkweather*

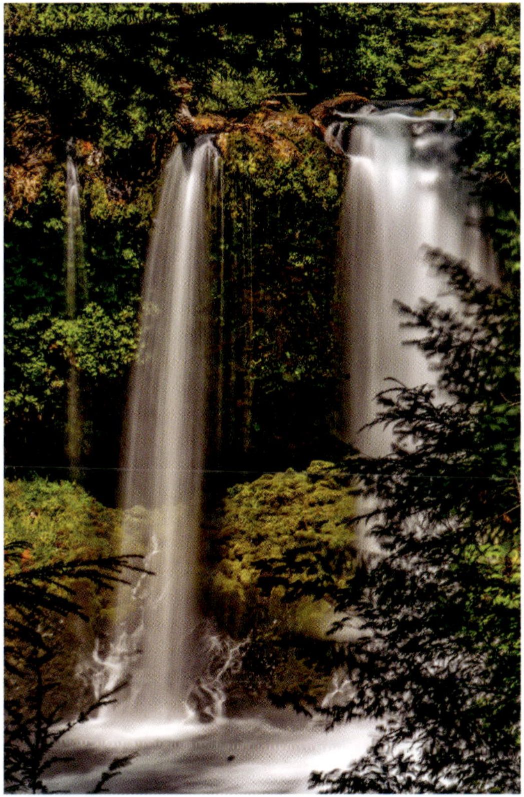

Koosah Falls on the McKenzie River.
Photo by George F. Peterson

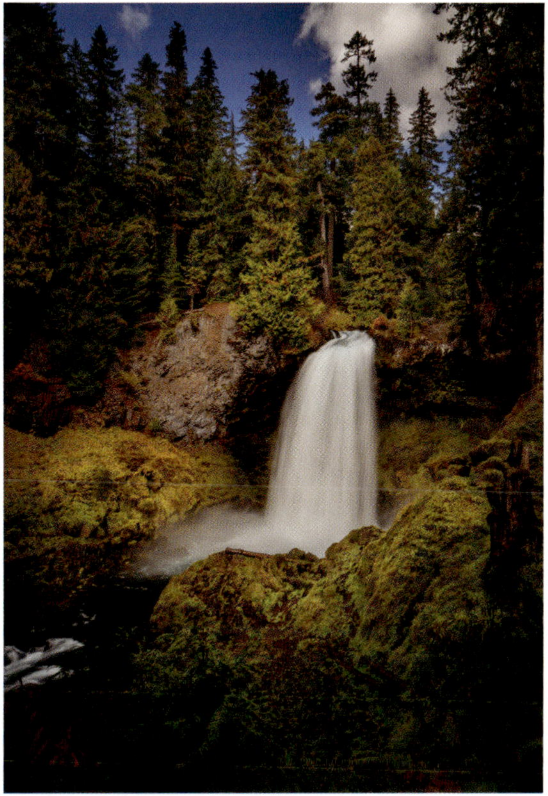

Sahalie Falls. *Photo by Alana Lynn Starkweather*

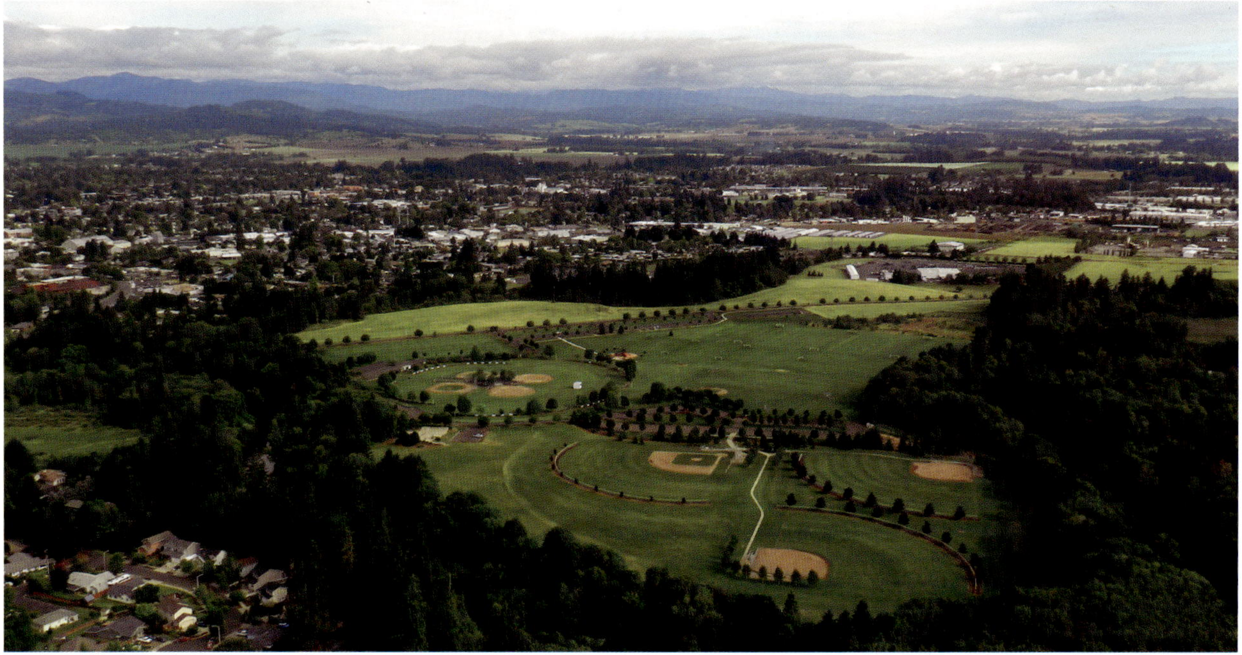

Joe Dancer Park, McMinnville.
Photo by Charles Hillestad

Hazelnut trees. *Photo by John Kirk*

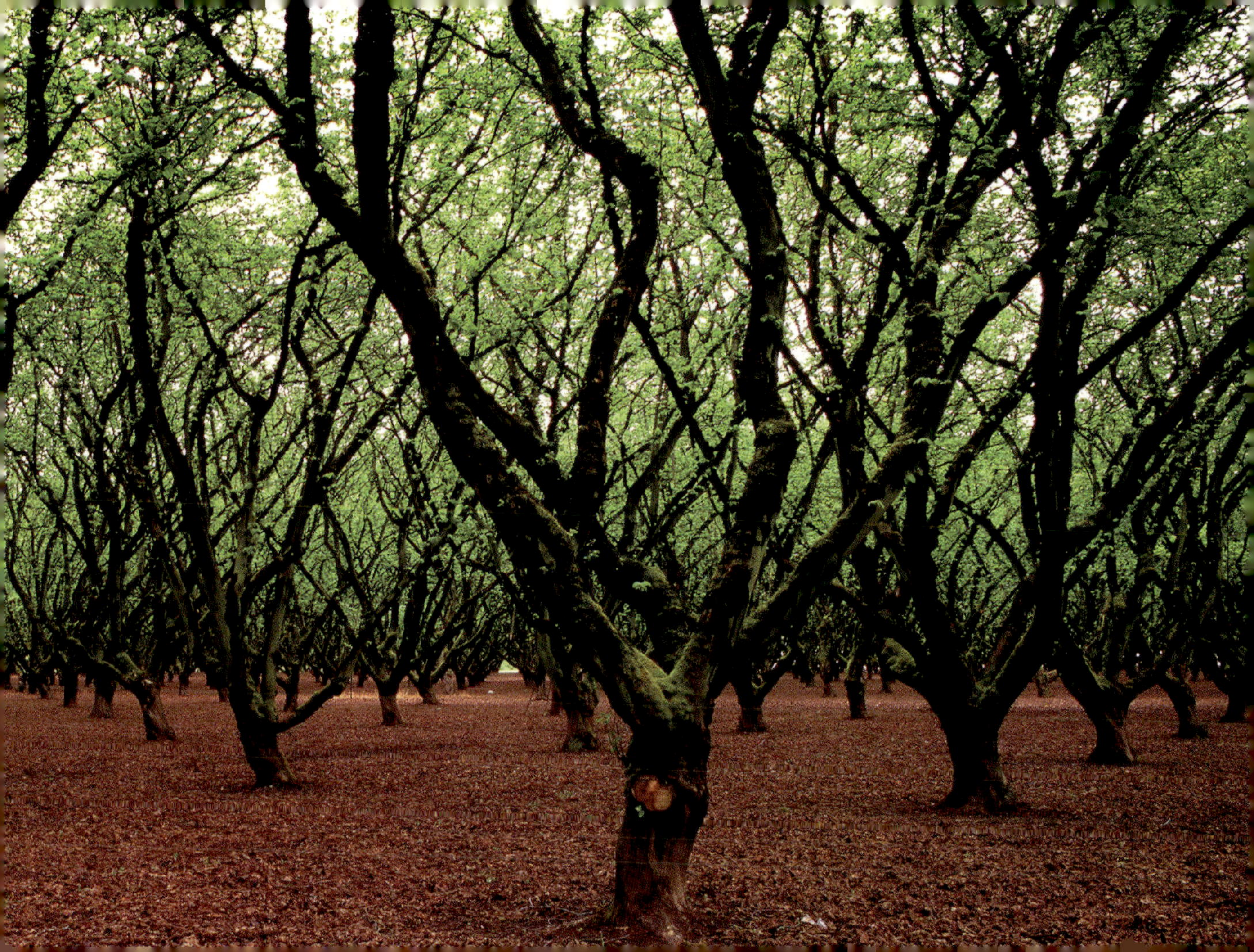

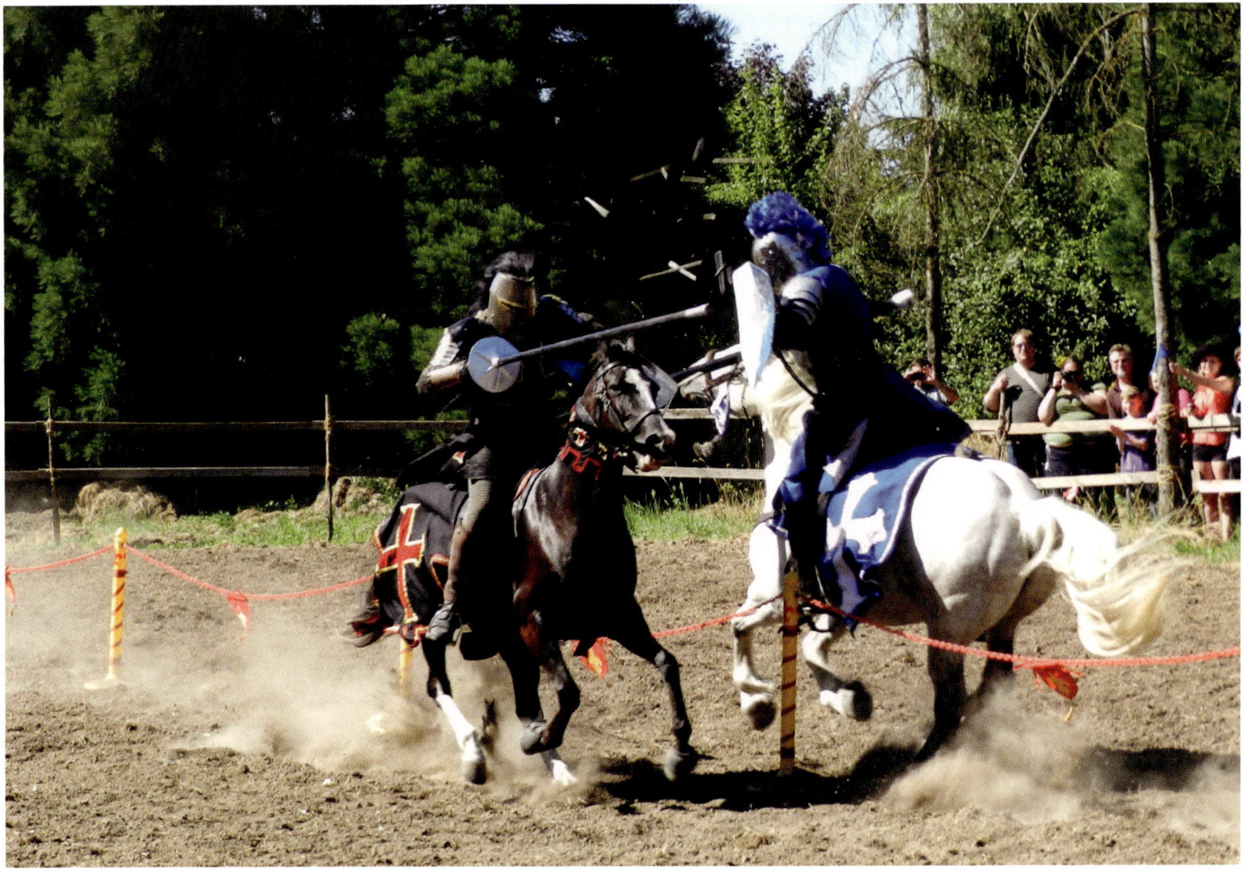

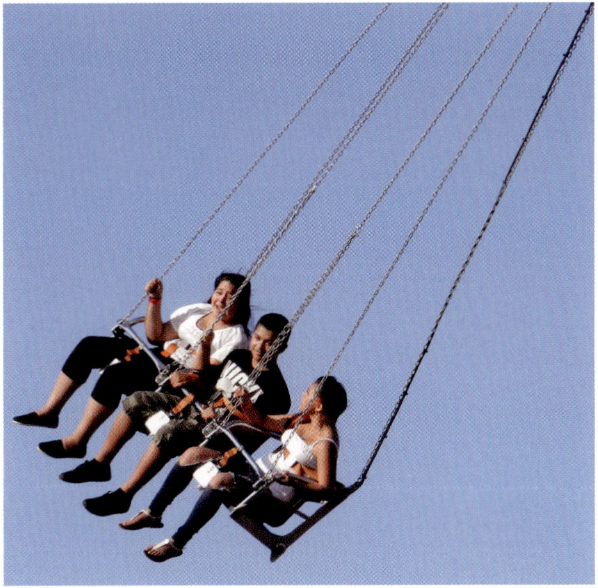

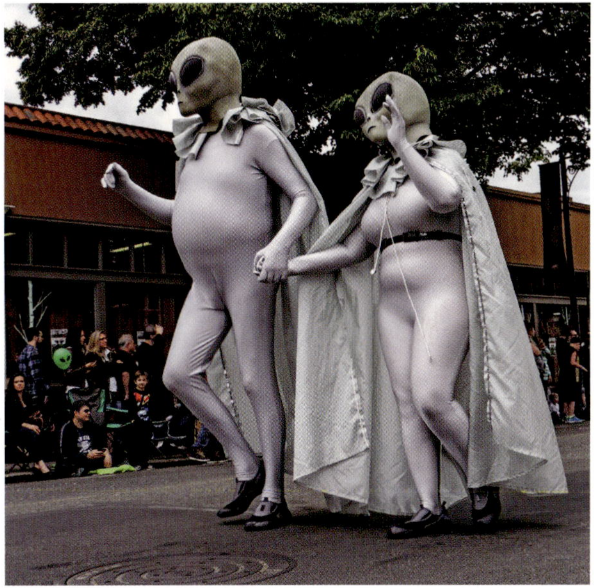

Jousting at the Canterbury Renaissance Faire near Silverton. *Photo by Charles Hillestad*

Carnival ride at McMinnville's TurkeyRama Festival. *Photo by Charles Hillestad*

Annual Alien Days Parade, McMinnville. *Photo by Charles Hillestad*

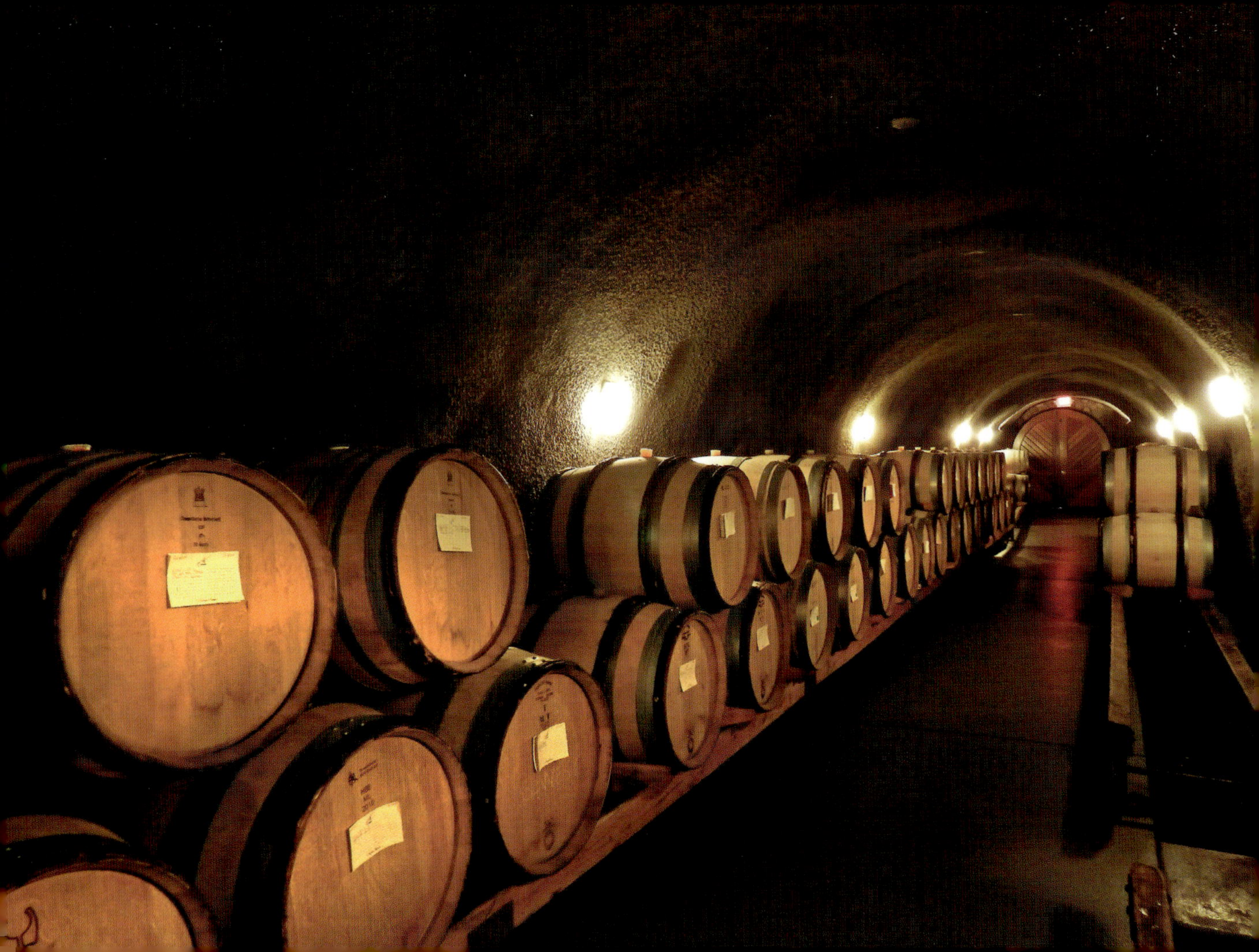

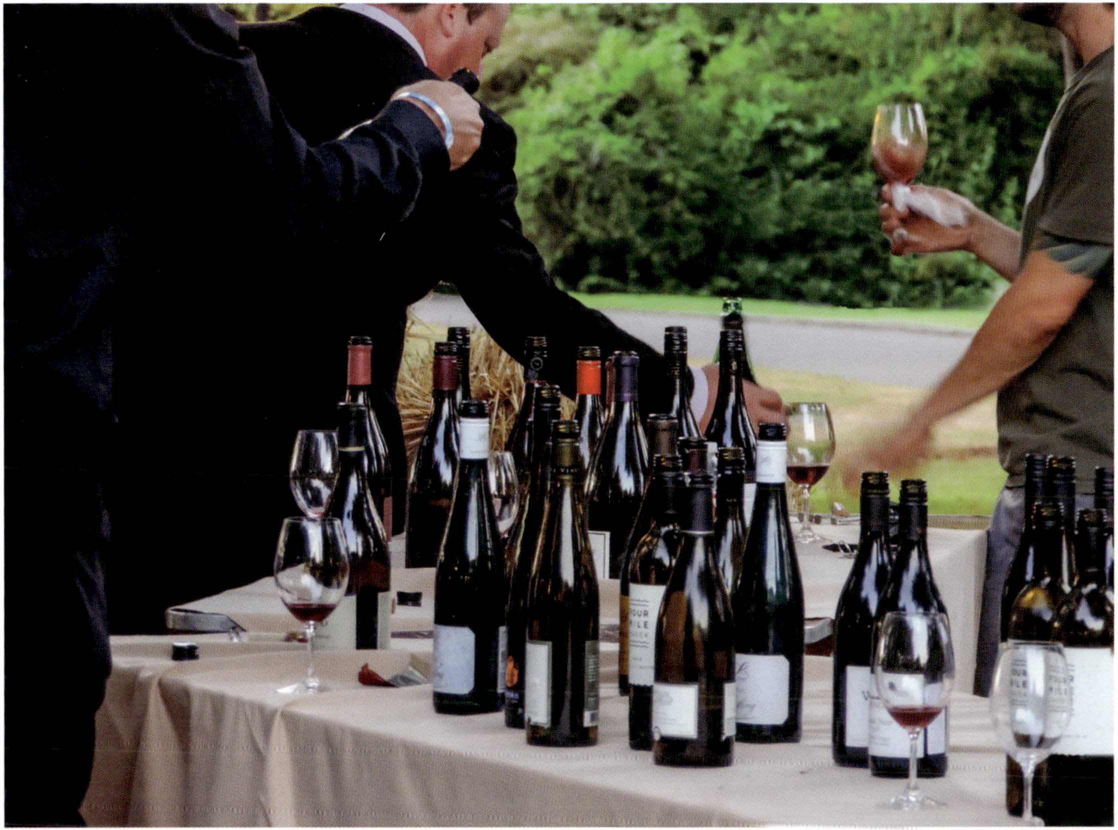

Archery Summit Winery Barrel Cave, Dayton.
Photo by Charles Hillestad

International Pinot Noir Festival at Linfield College, Oak Grove. *Photo by Charles Hillestad*

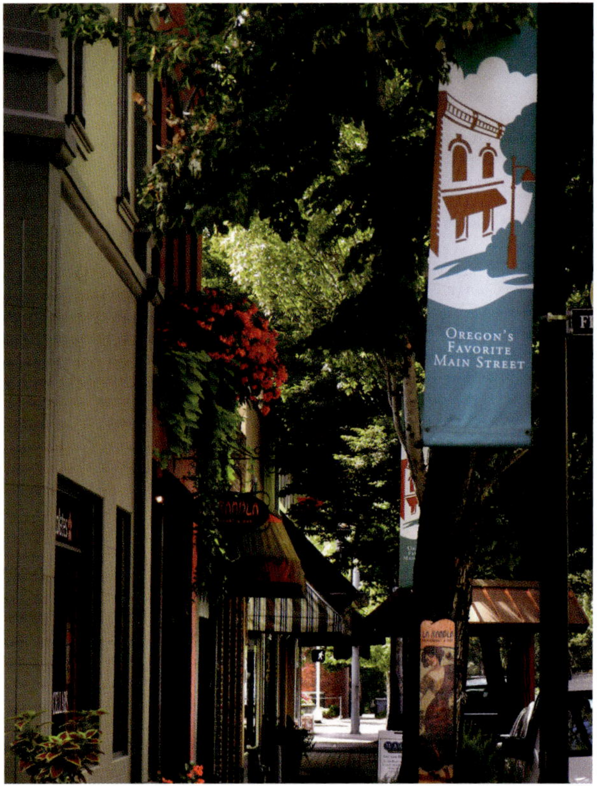

Historic downtown McMinnville, "Oregon's Favorite Main Street." *Photo by Charles Hillestad*

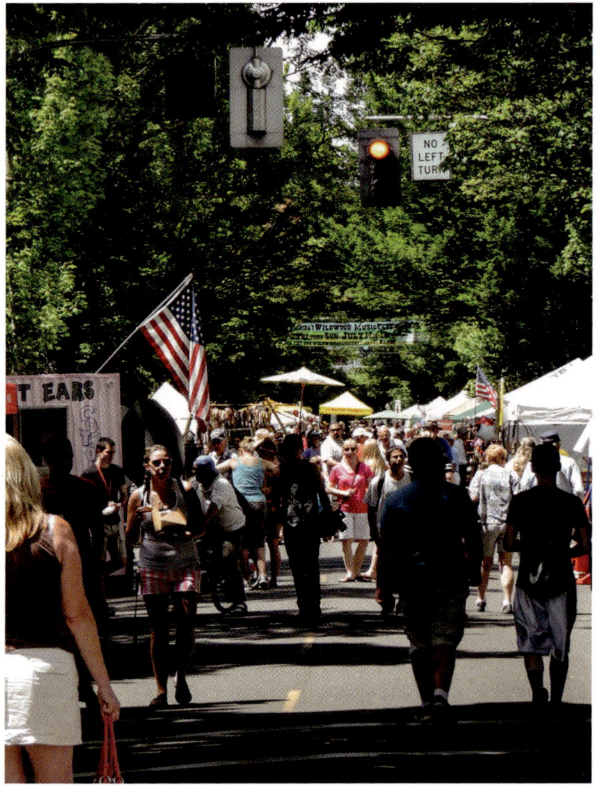

TurkeyRama, under McMinnville's tunnel of trees. *Photo by Charles Hillestad*

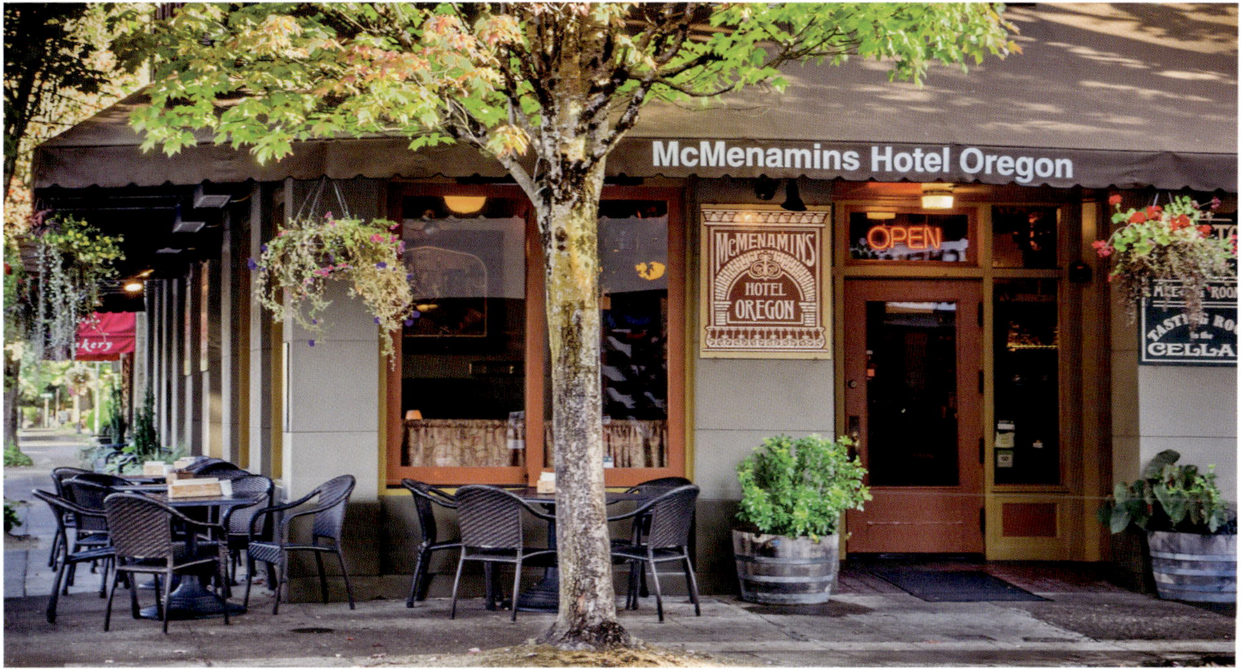

McMenamins Historic Hotel Oregon, McMinnville, since 1905.
Photo by George F. Peterson

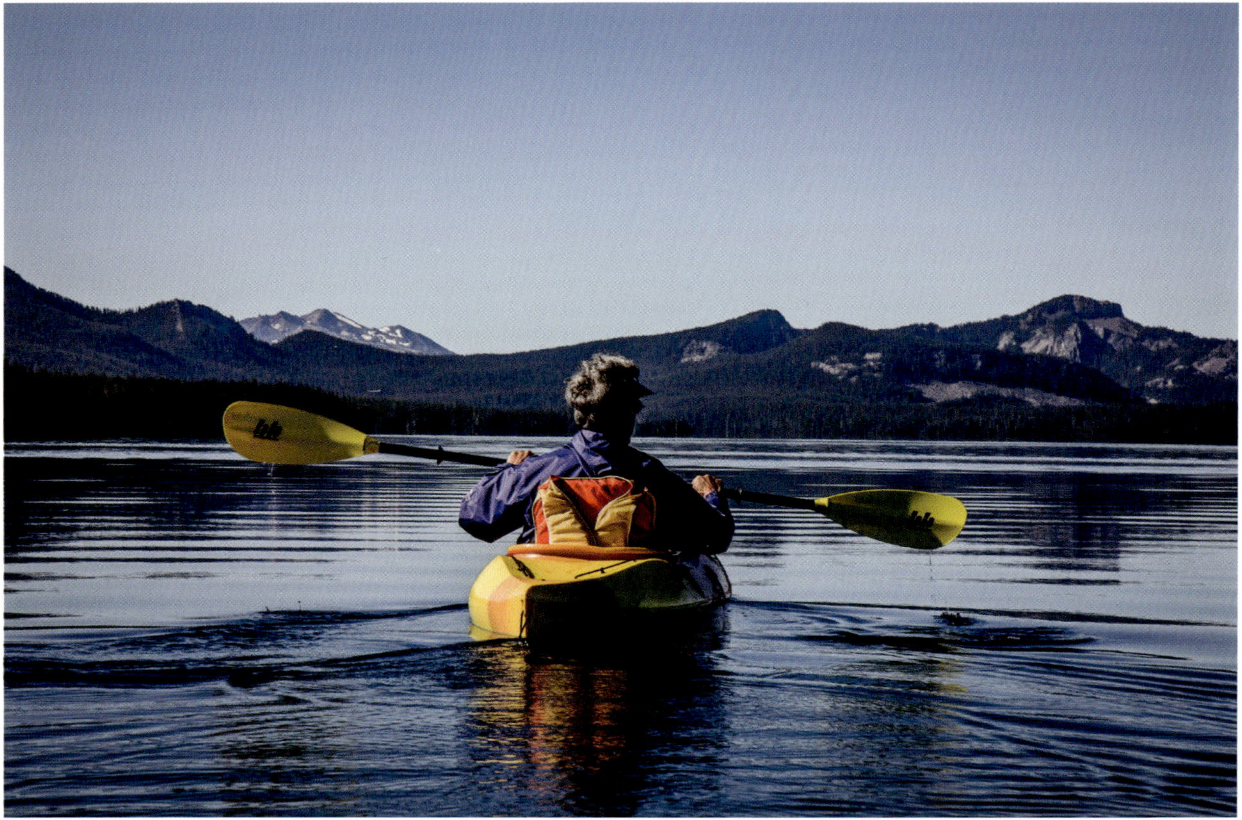

Waldo Lake. *Photo by Kate Geary*

Sunflower field. *Photo by Vivian McAleavey*

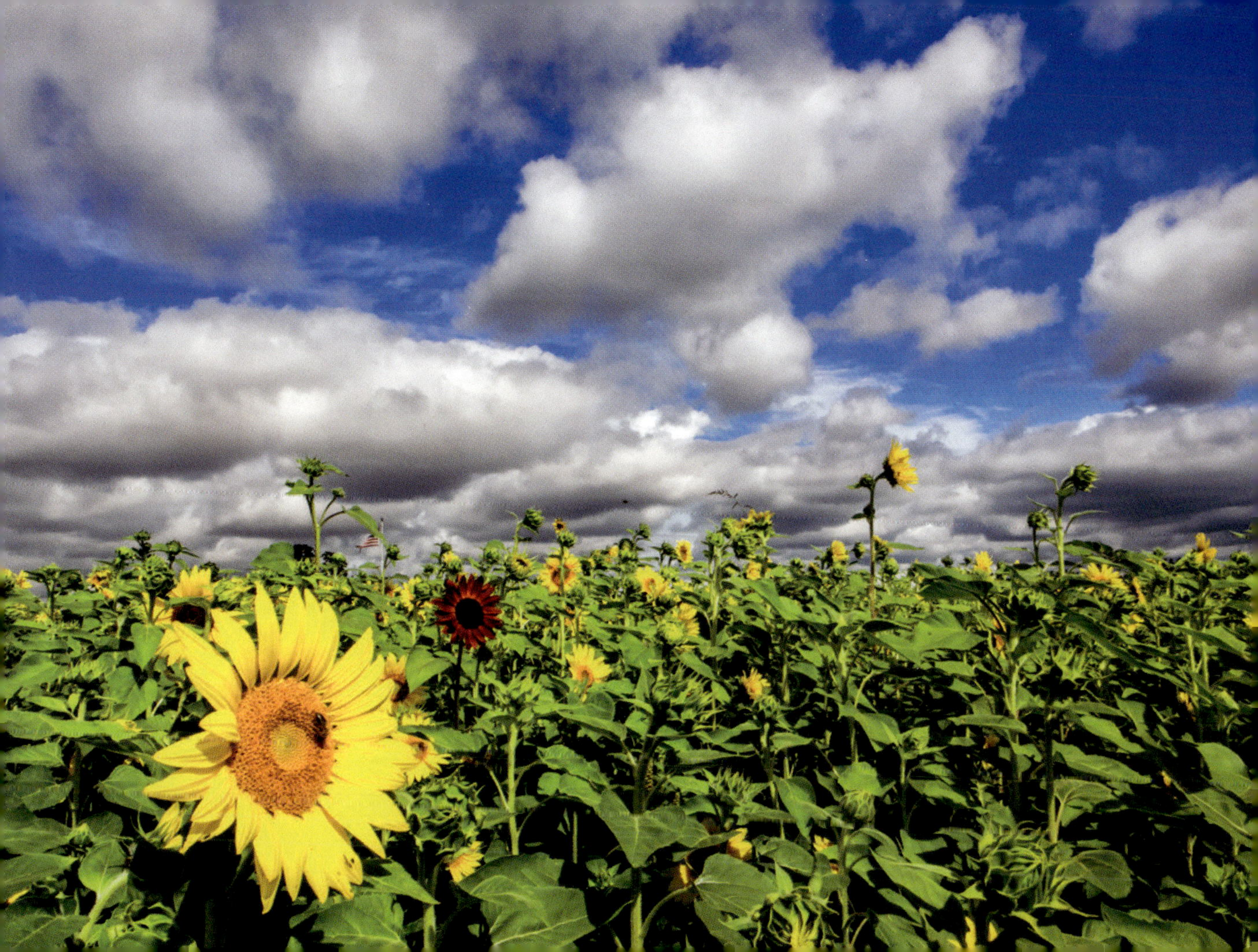

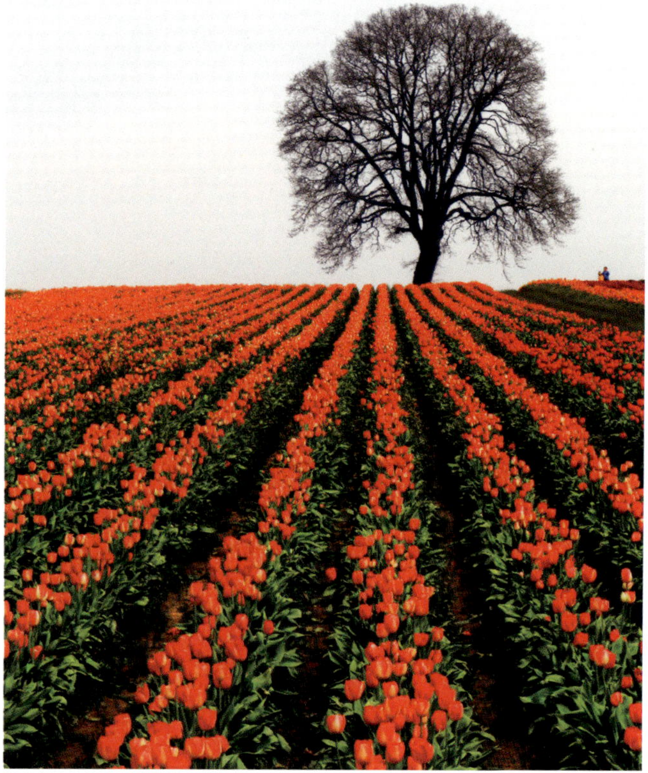

Wooden Shoe Tulip Festival, Woodburn.
Photo by Charles Hillestad

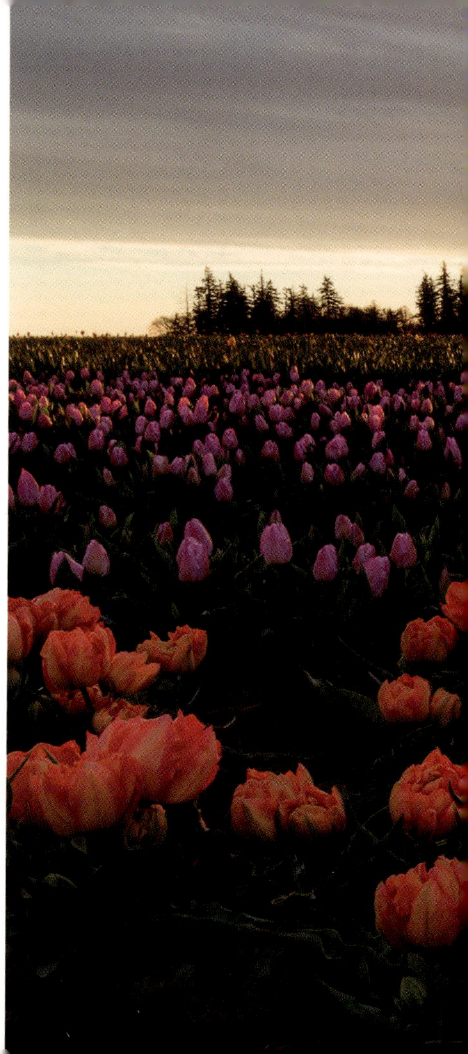

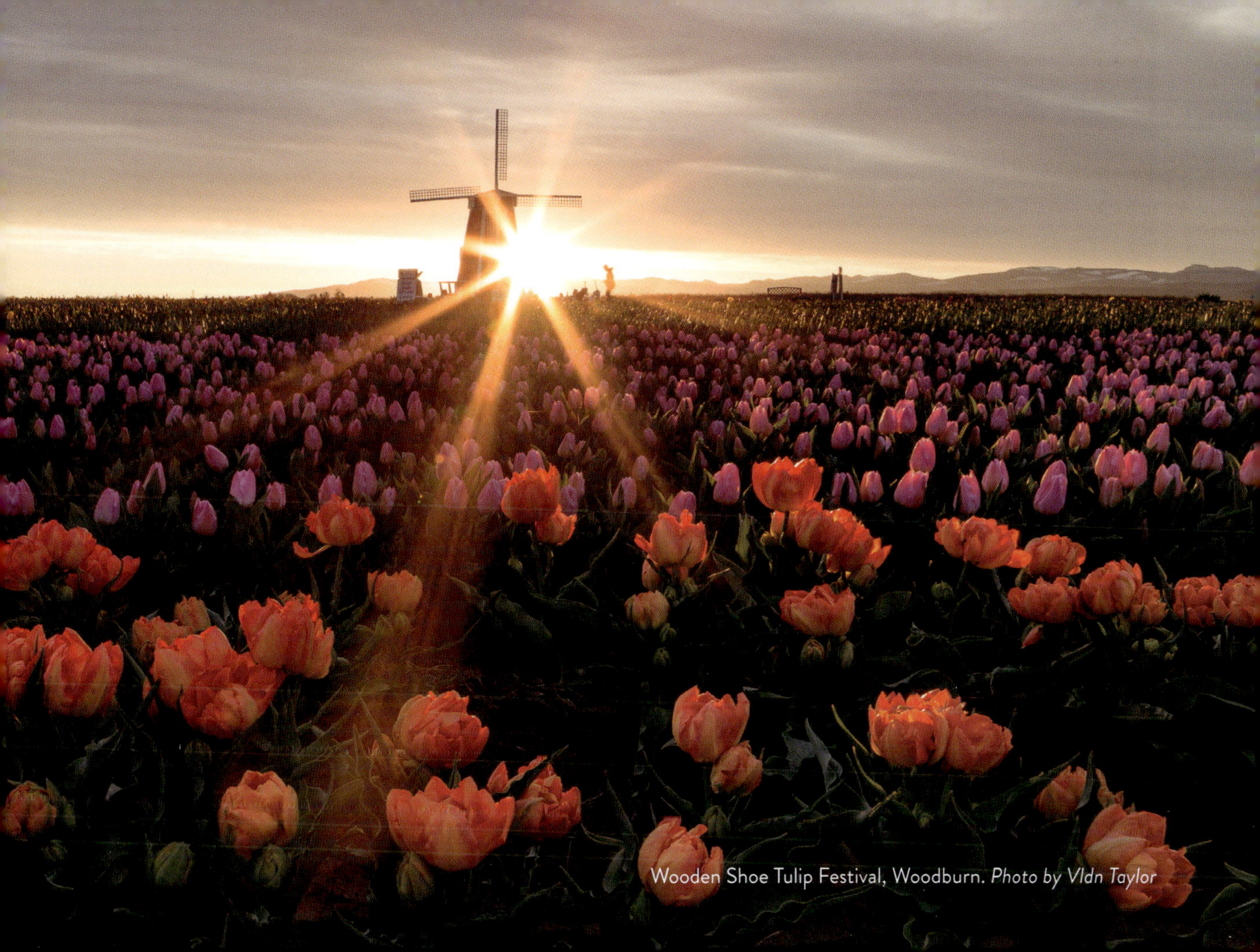

Wooden Shoe Tulip Festival, Woodburn. *Photo by Vldn Taylor*

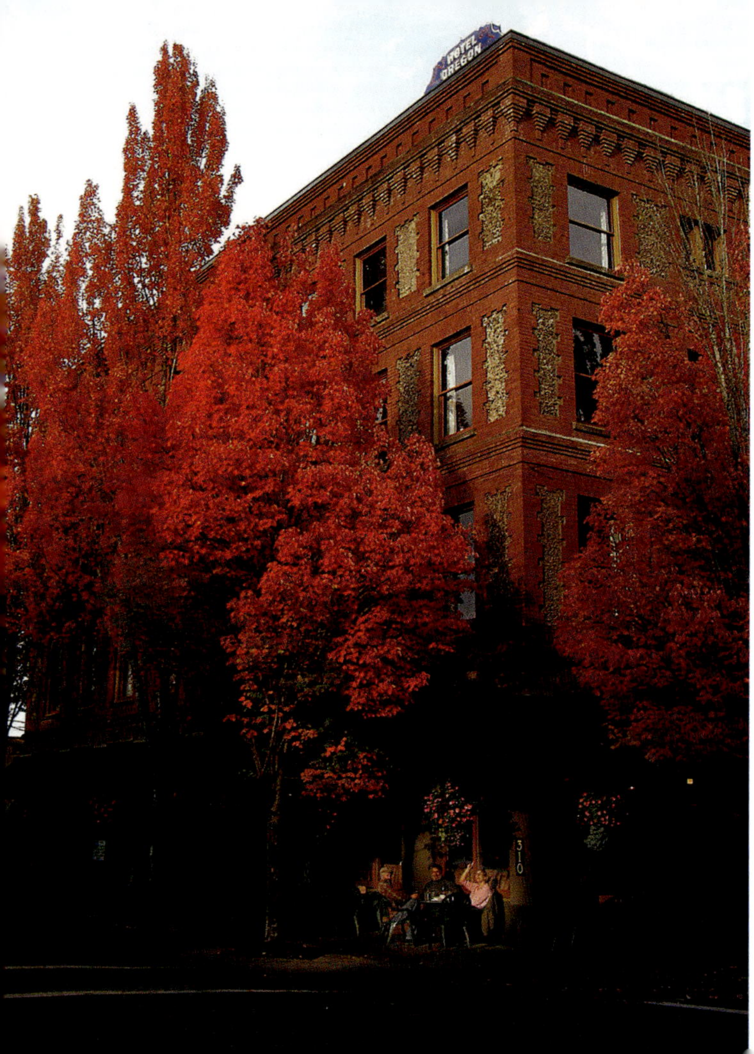

McMenamins Historic Hotel Oregon, McMinnville.
Photo by Charles Hillestad

Deepwood Museum & Gardens, Salem, built in 1893. *Photo by Howard Hunt*

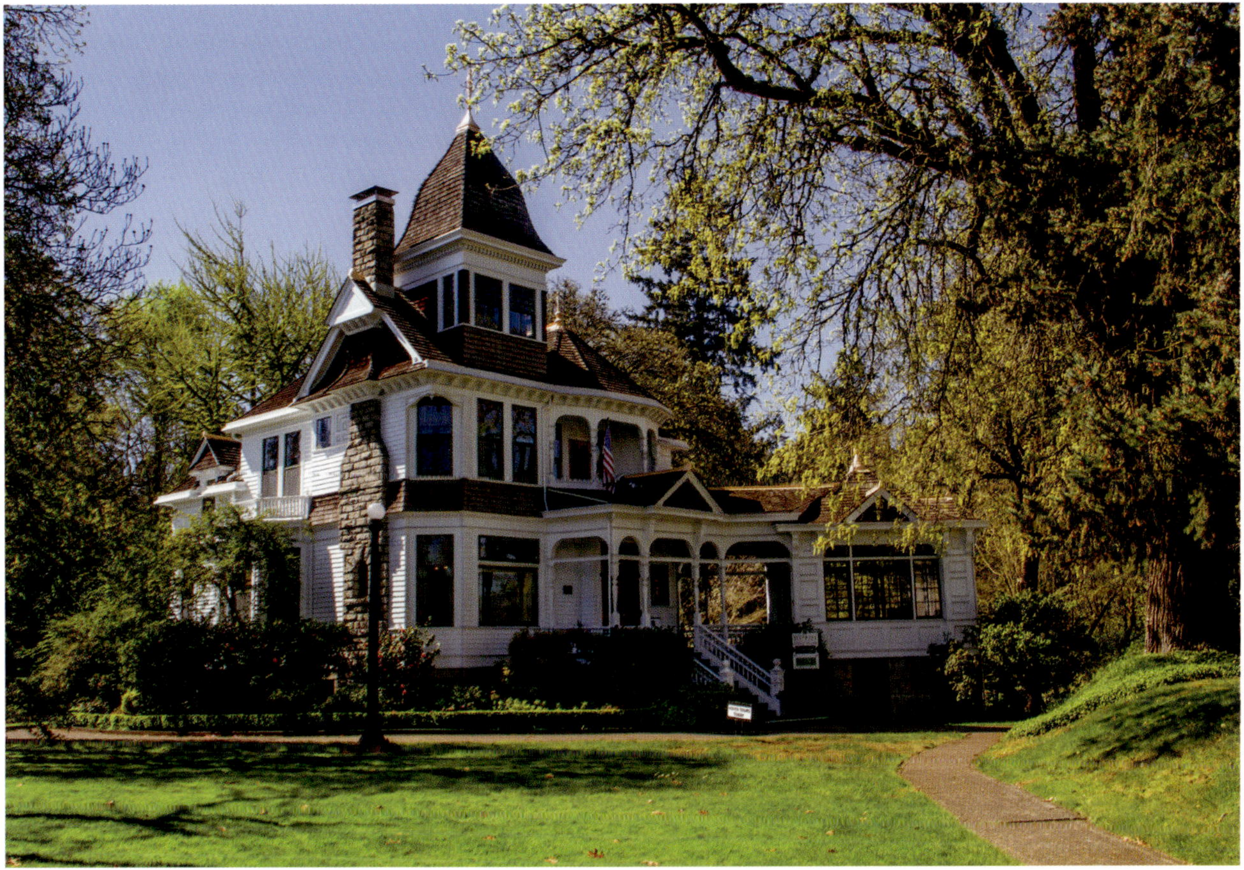

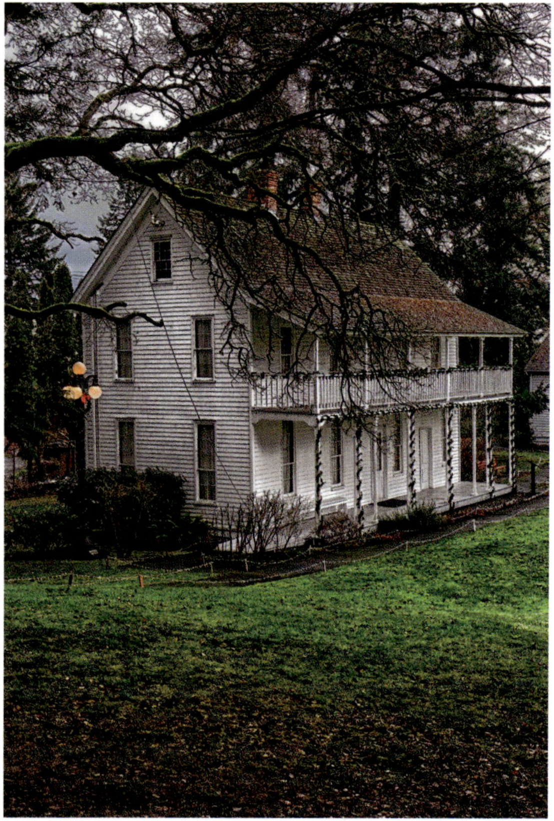

Lee House, Willamette Heritage Center, Salem.
Photo by Richard Krieger

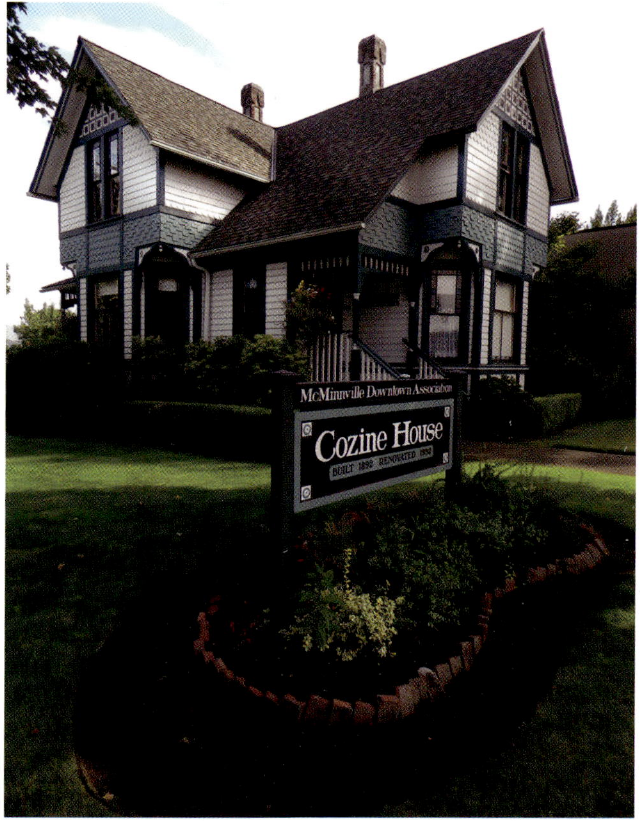

Samuel Cozine House, built in 1892, McMinnville.
Photo by Charles Hillestad

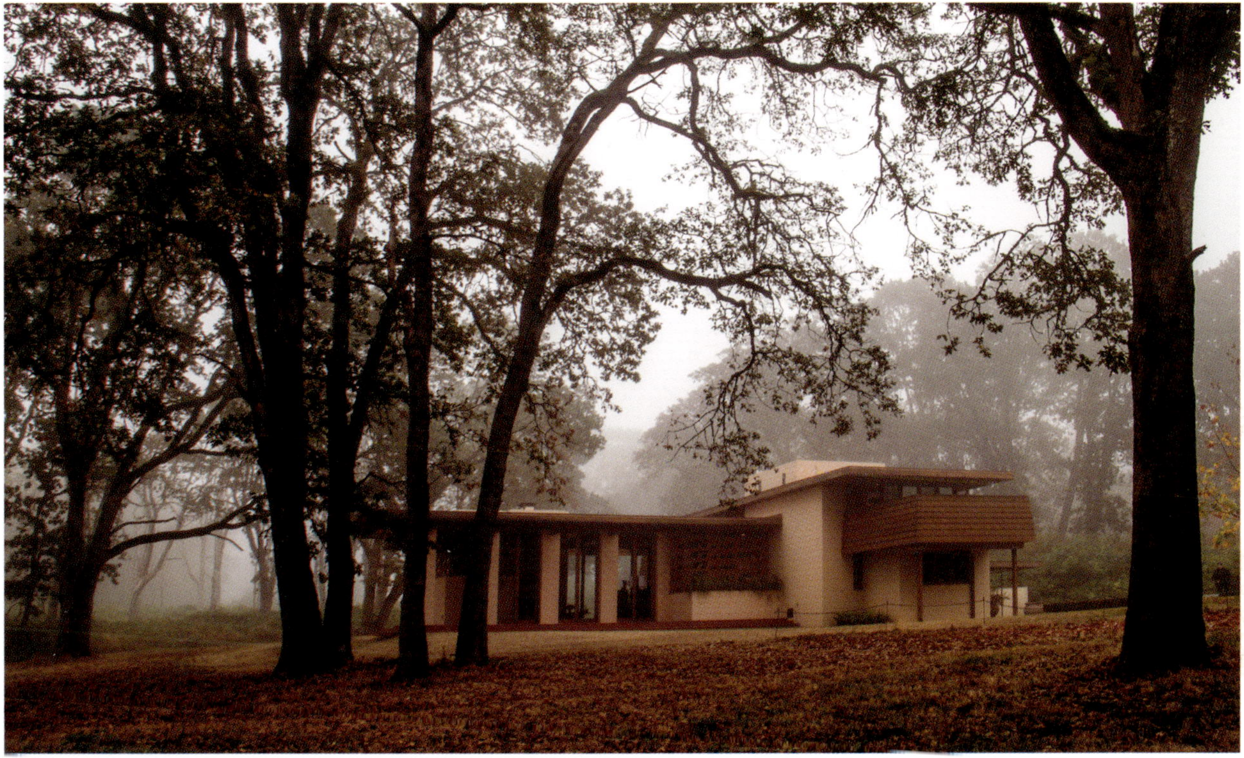

The C. E. Gordon House is the only Frank Lloyd Wright house in Oregon. It was built in 1957 in Wilsonville and relocated to Silverton in 2001. *Photo by Howard Hunt*

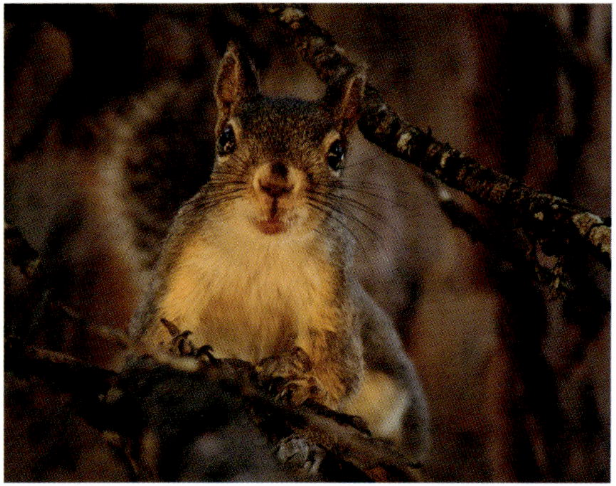

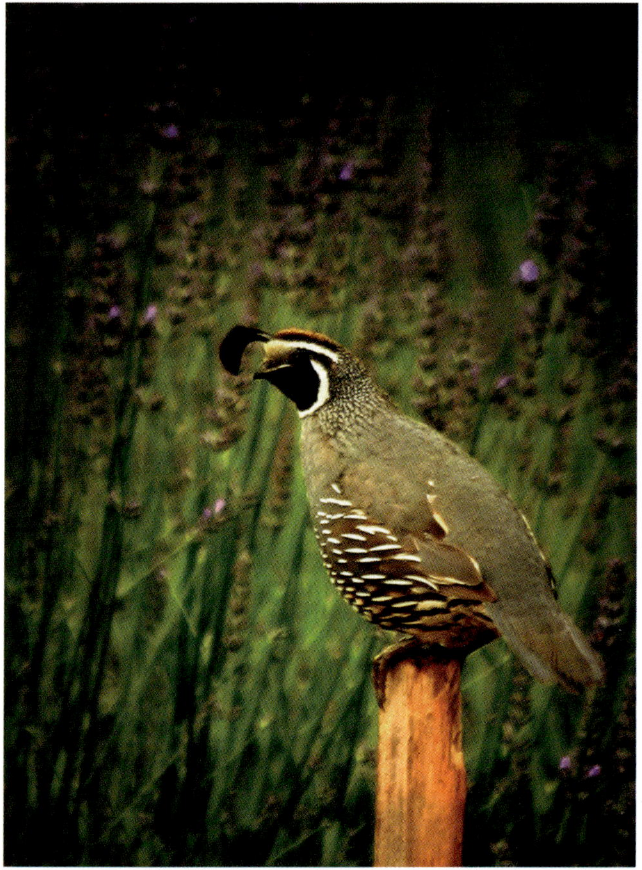

Squirrel on watch duty. *Photo by John Kirk*

Quail. *Photo by John Kirk*

Oregon Gardens reflective tree ponds, Silverton.
Photo by John Christer Petersen

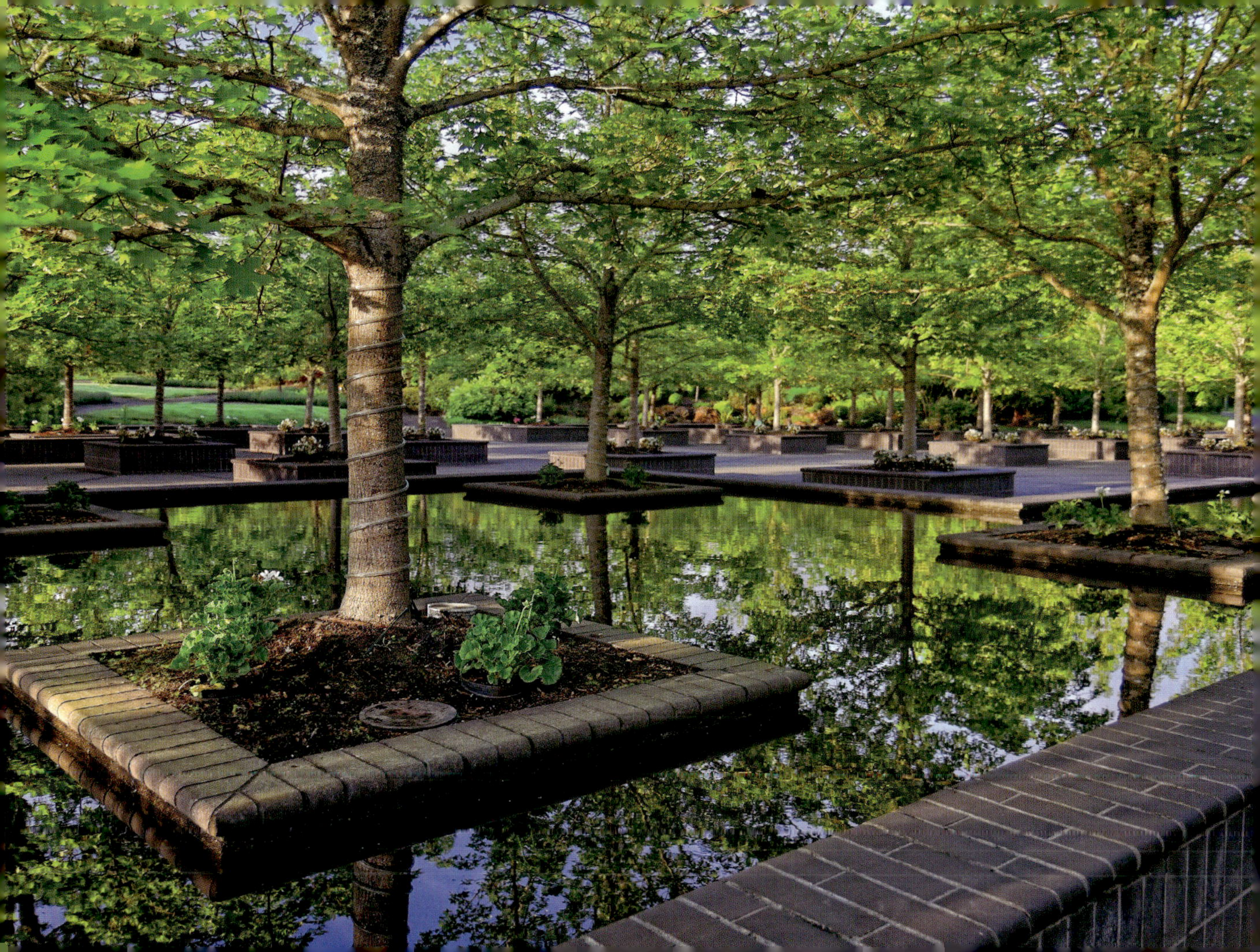

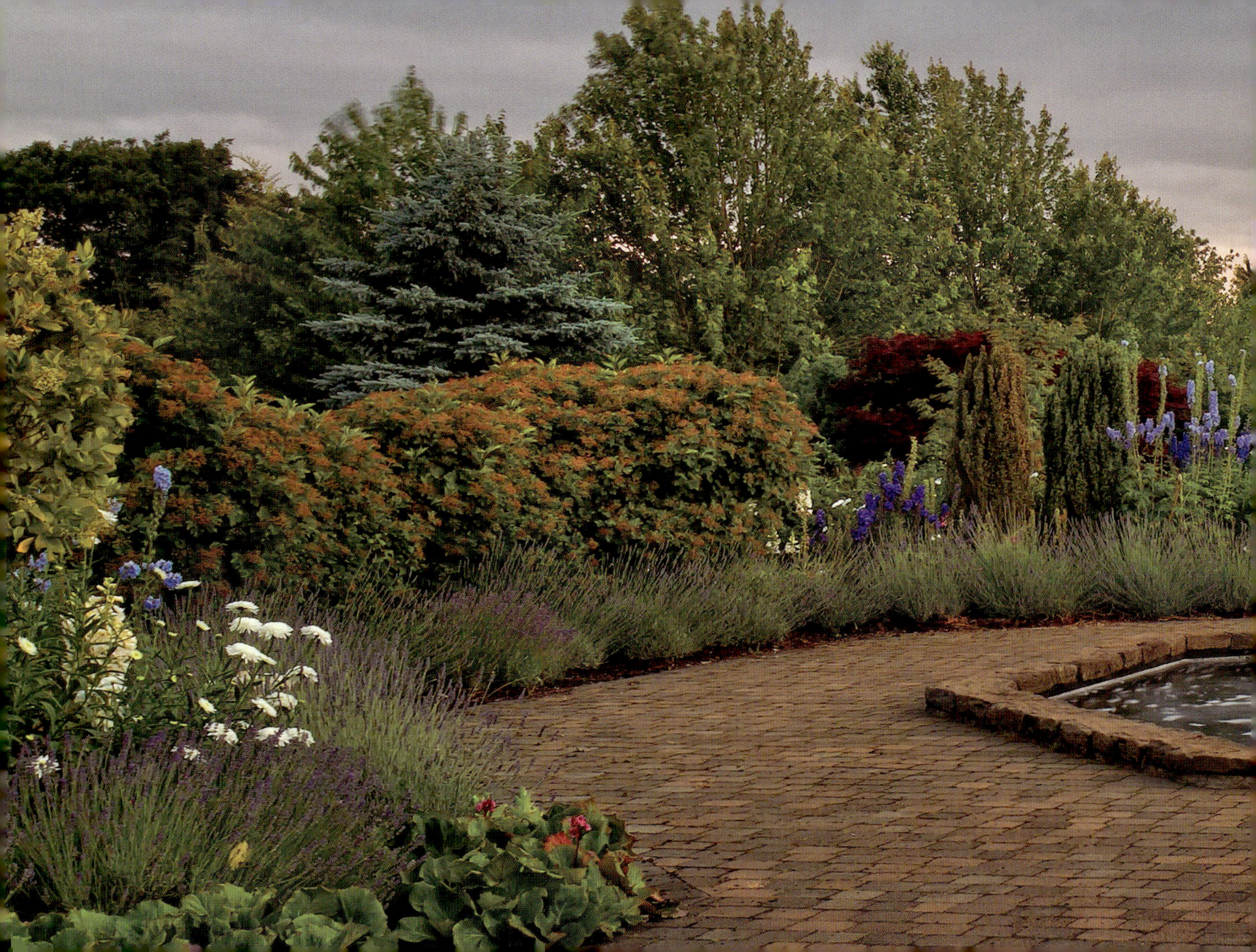

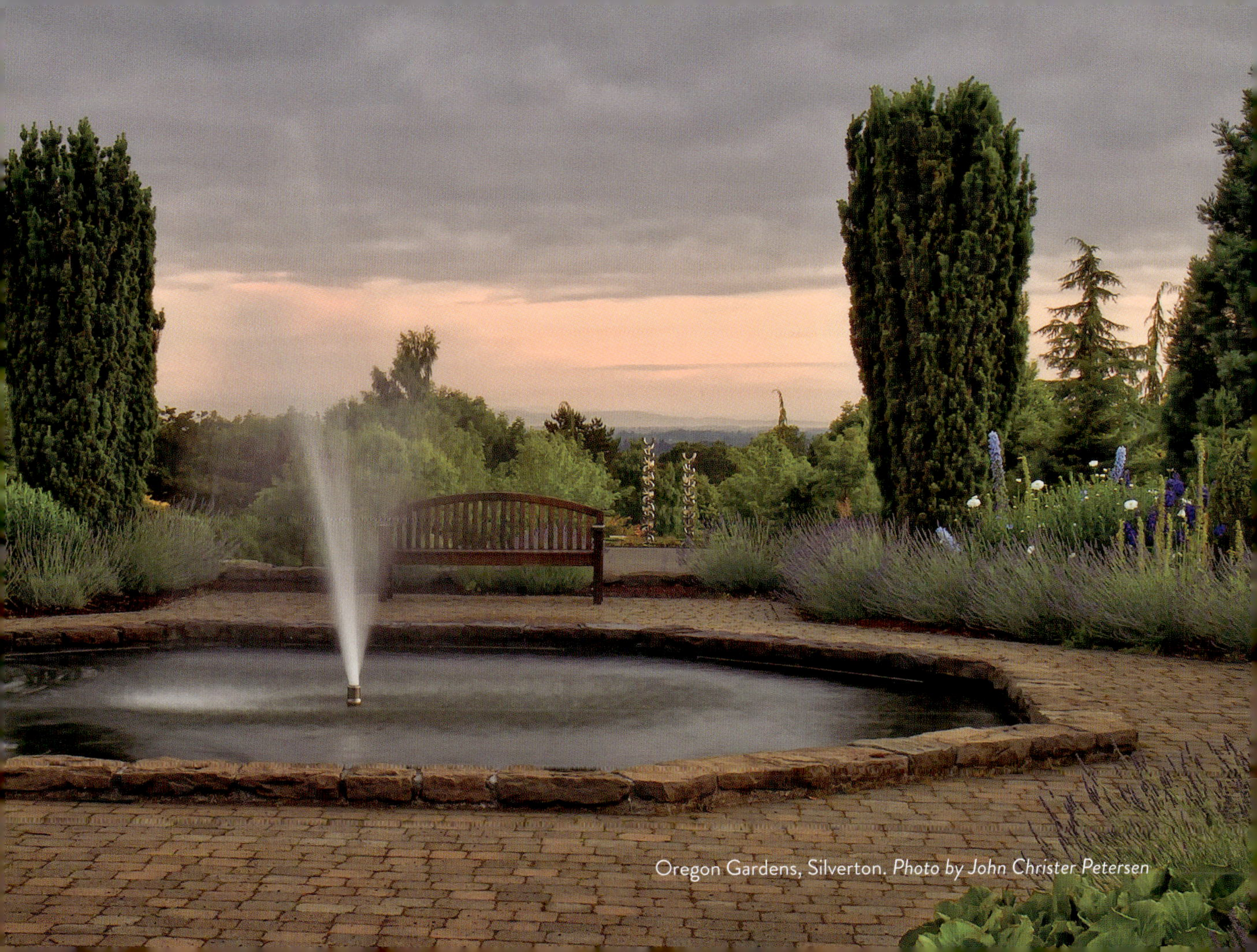

Oregon Gardens, Silverton. *Photo by John Christer Petersen*

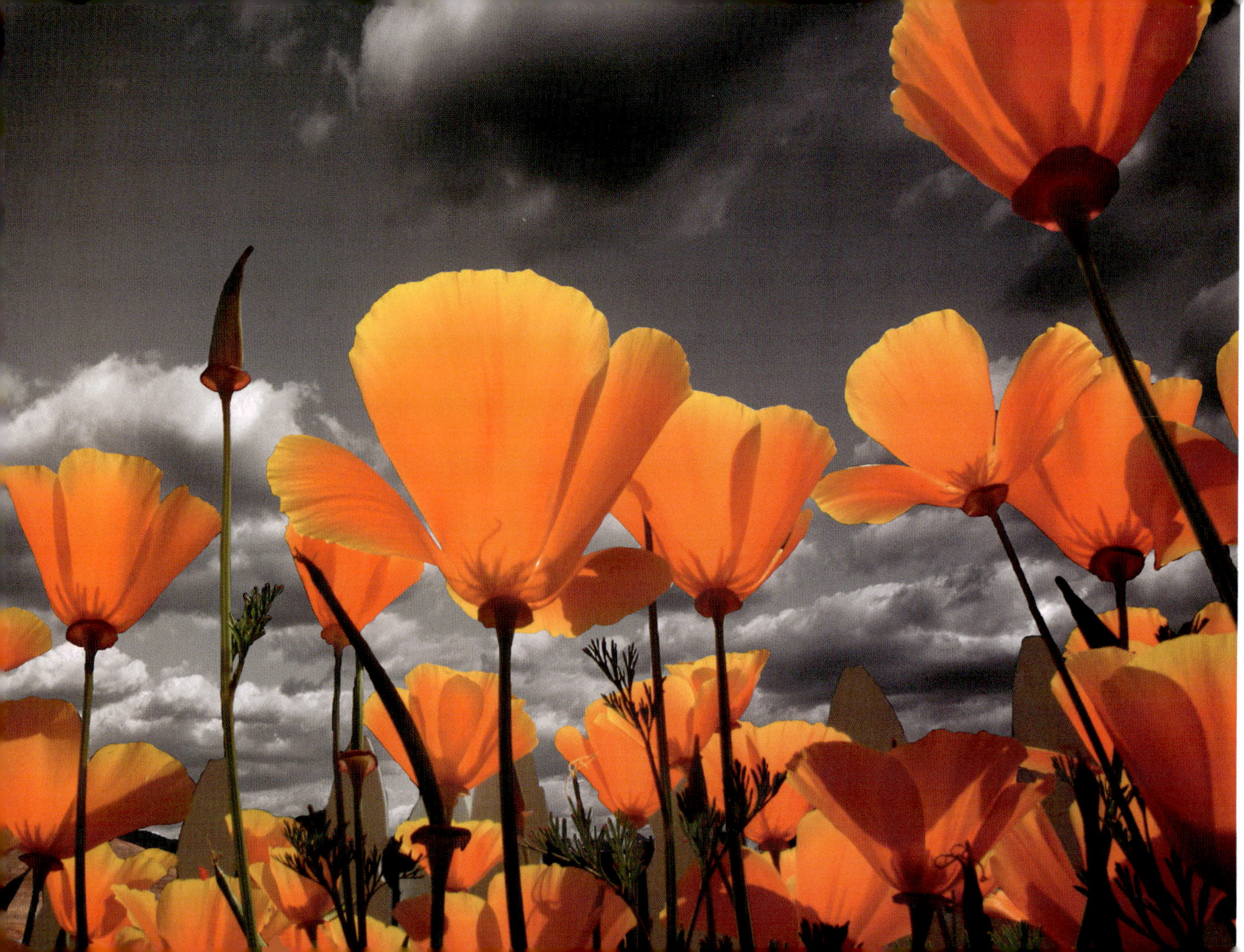

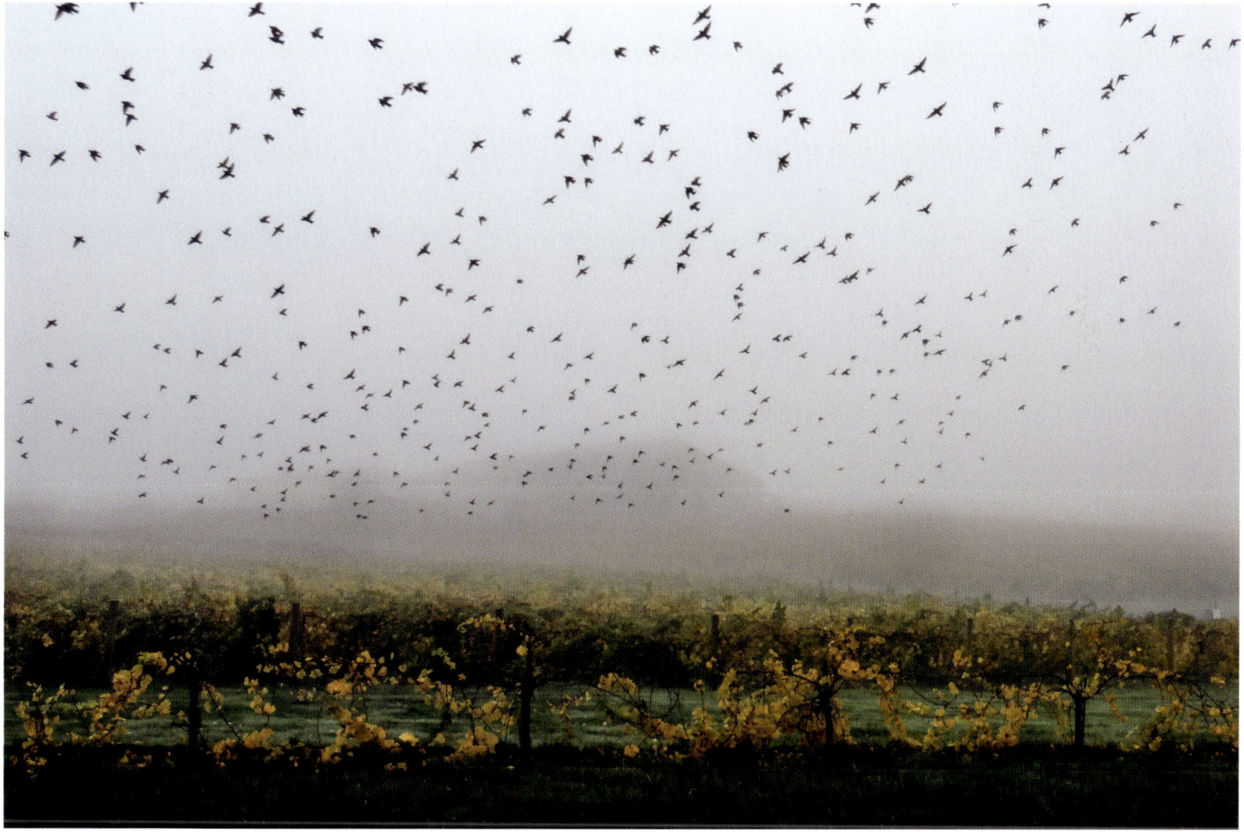

Poppy field. *Photo by John Kirk*

Starlings in vineyard. *Photo by Charles Hillestad*

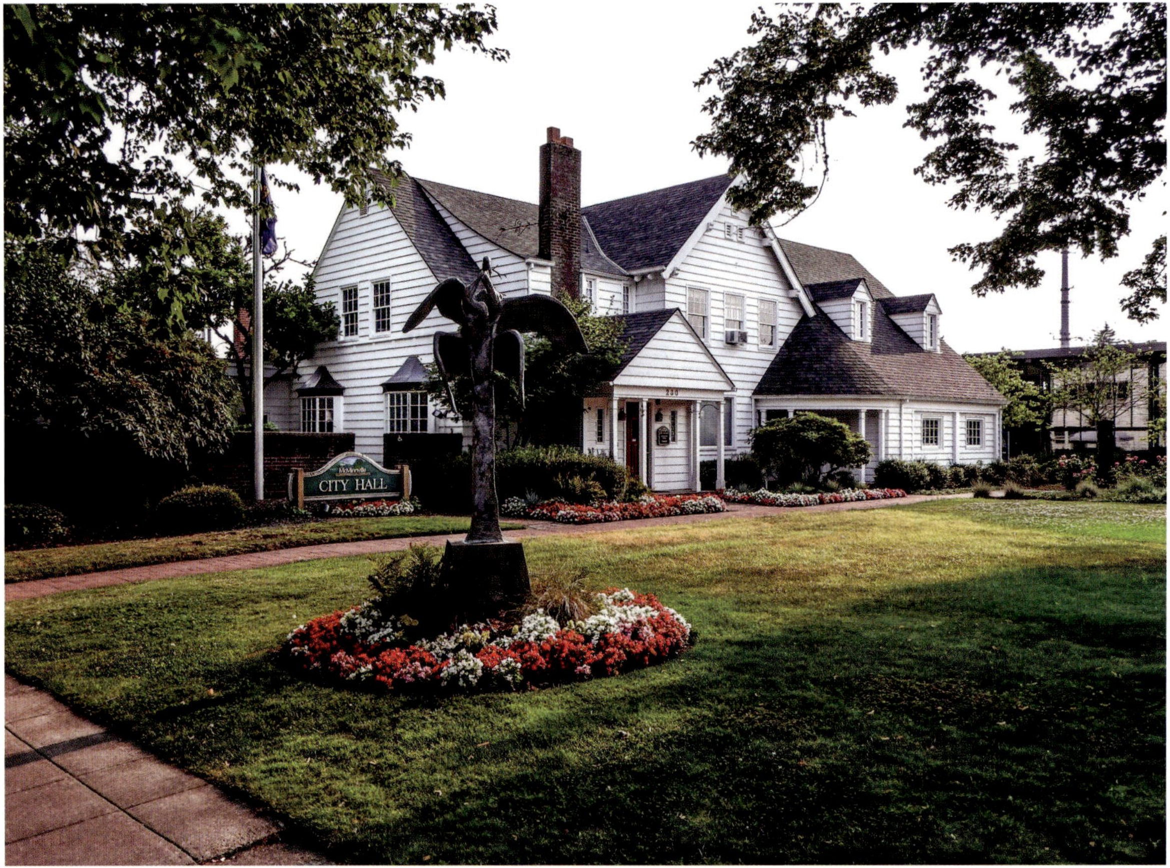
McMinnville
CITY HALL

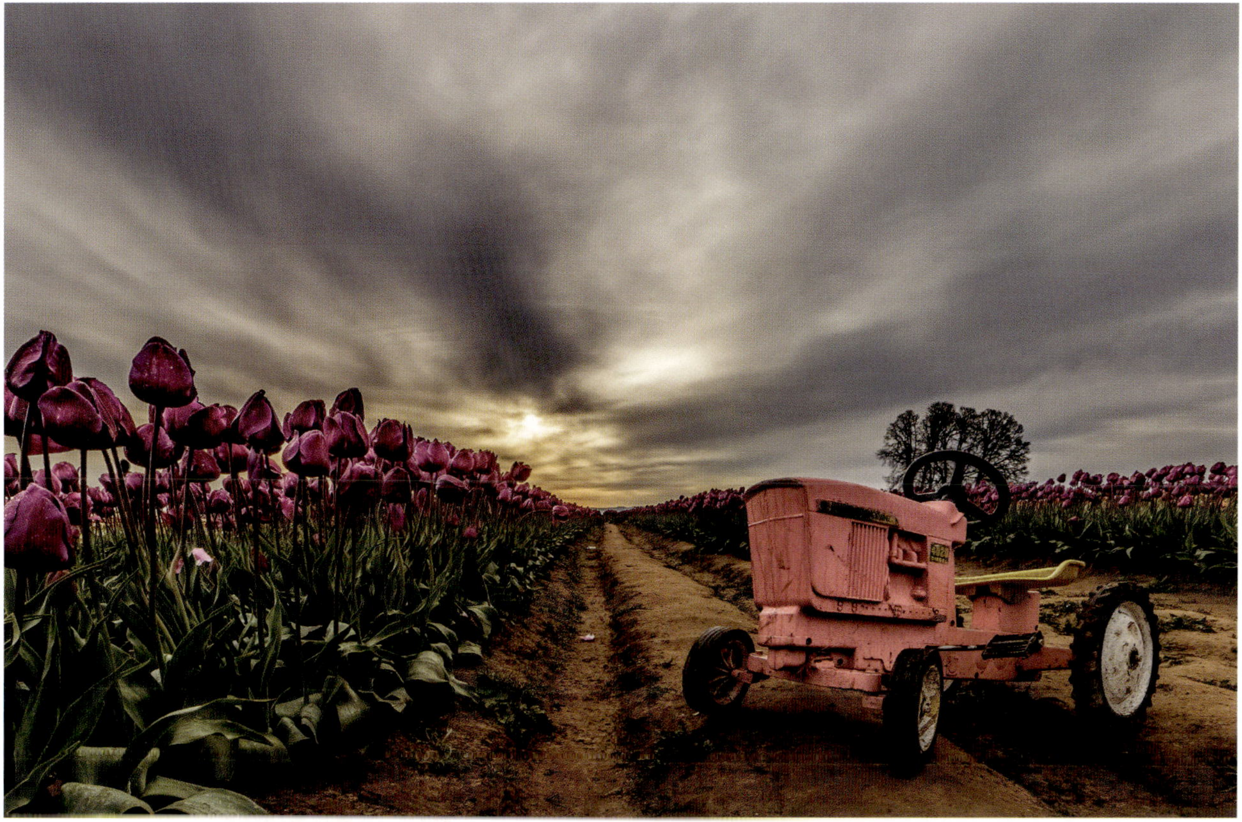

McMinnville City Hall. *Photo by Charles Hillestad*

Wooden Shoe Tulip Festival, Woodburn. *Photo by Vldn Taylor*

82

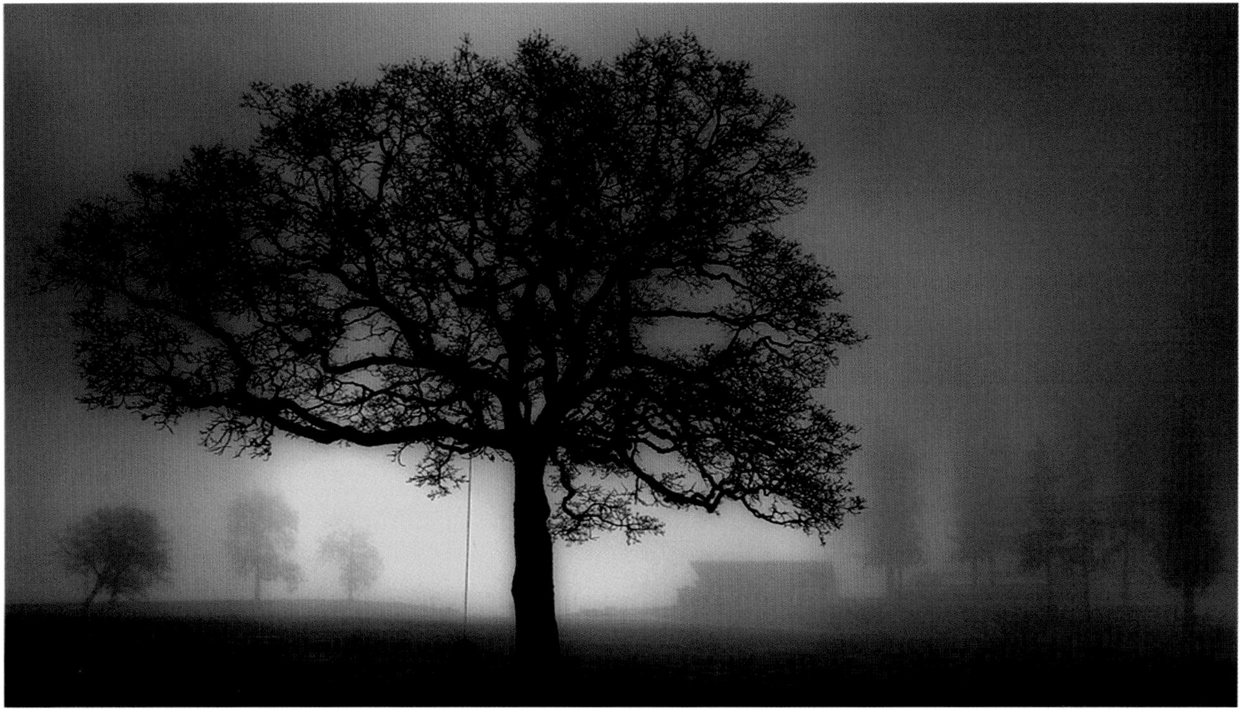

Foggy morning at a winery near Dayton.
Photo by Clem Paslack

Cottonwood grove south of McMinnville.
Photo by Charles Hillestad

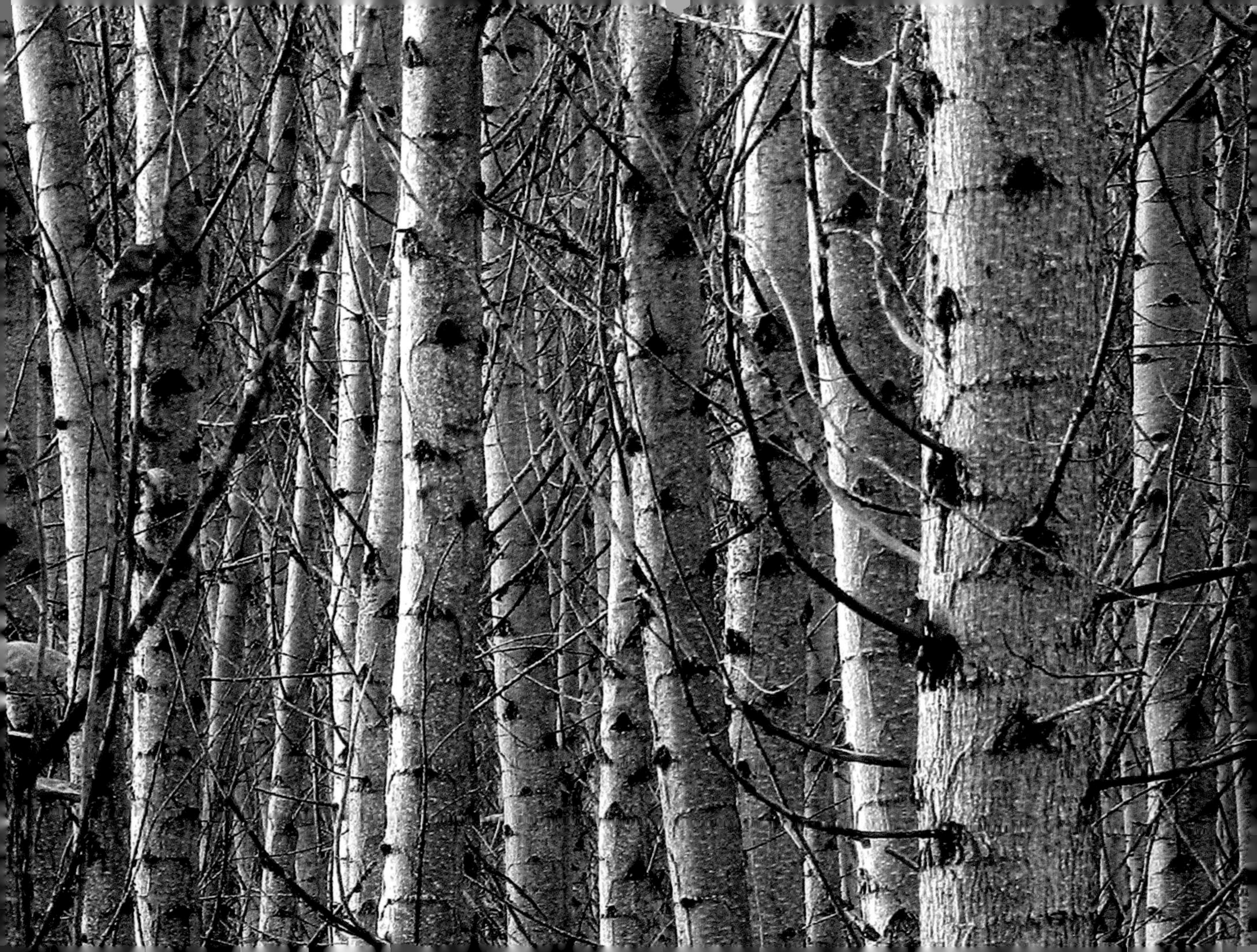

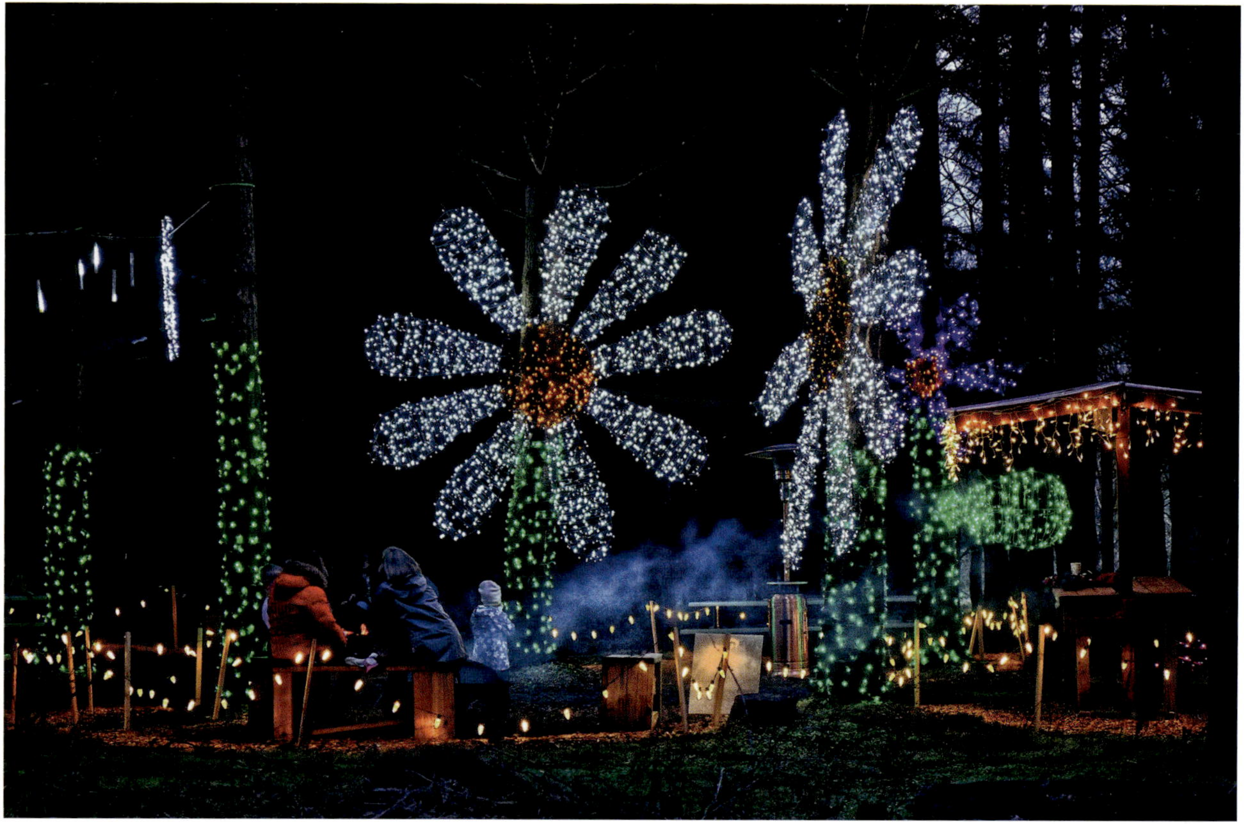

Christmas in the Garden at the Oregon Gardens, Silverton, is an annual winter festival with over a million lights. *Photo by Richard Krieger*

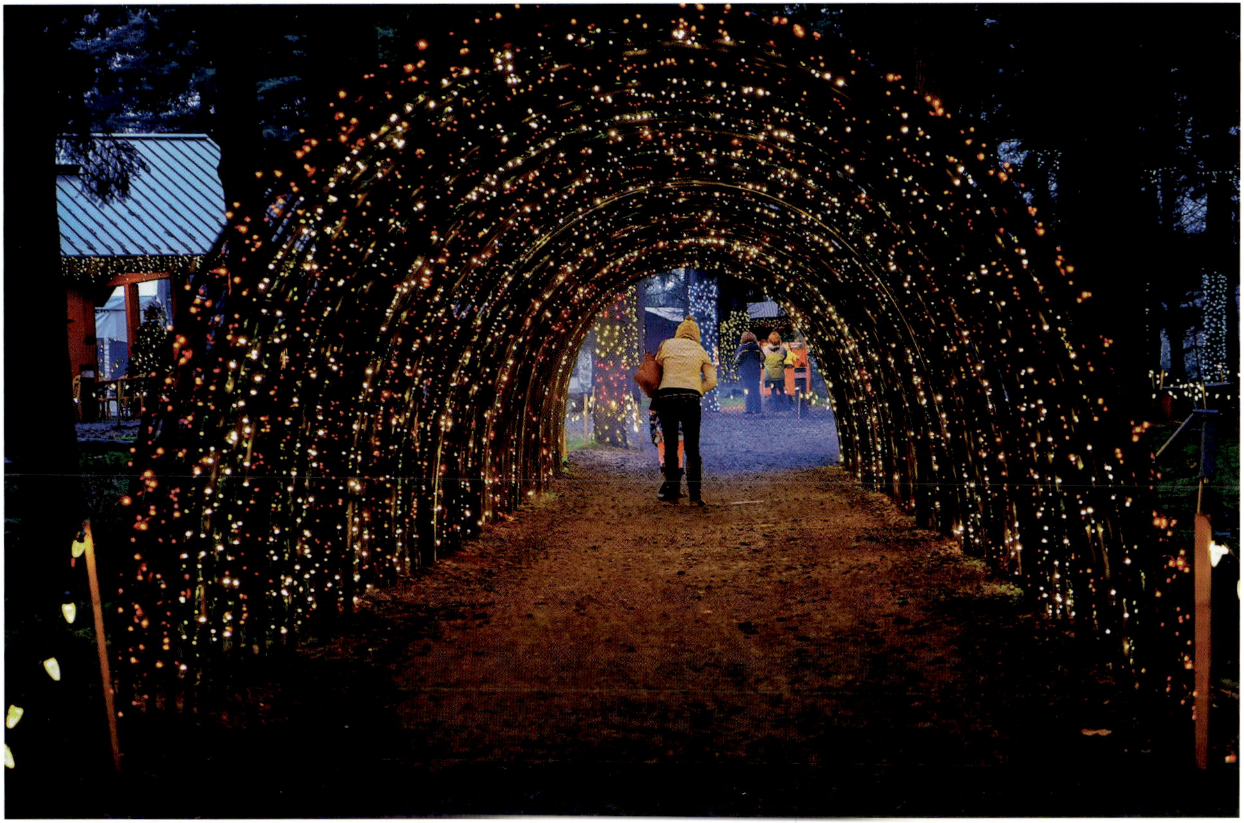

Candy Cane Tunnel at Christmas in the Garden,
Oregon Gardens, Silverton. *Photo by Richard Krieger*

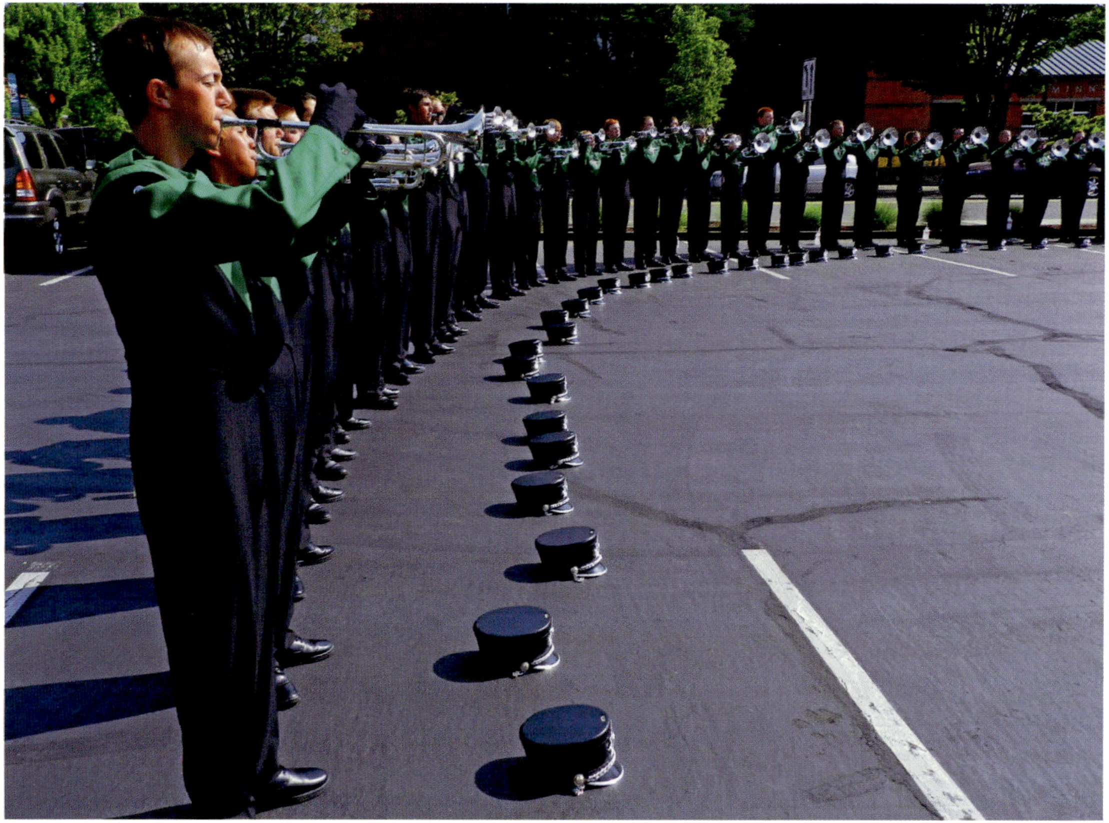

Practicing before a parade in McMinnville.
Photo by Charles Hillestad

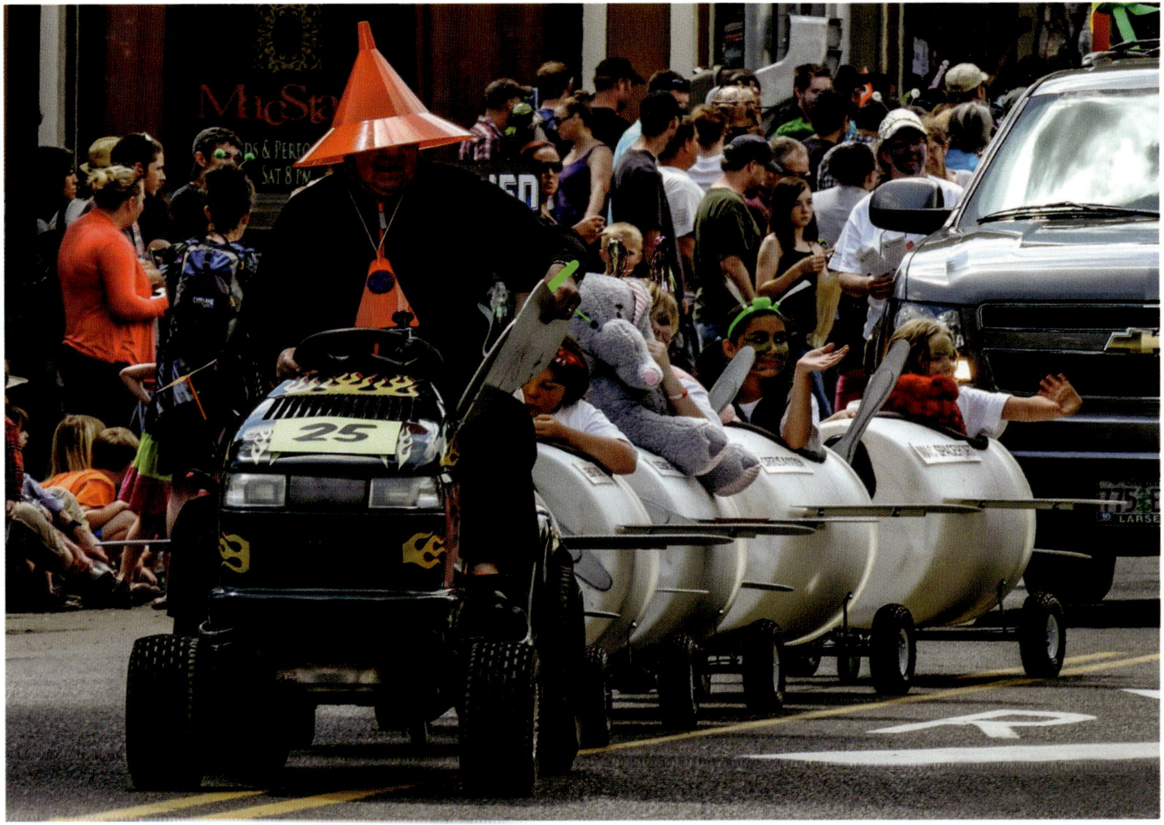

Parade in McMinnville. *Photo by Charles Hillestad*

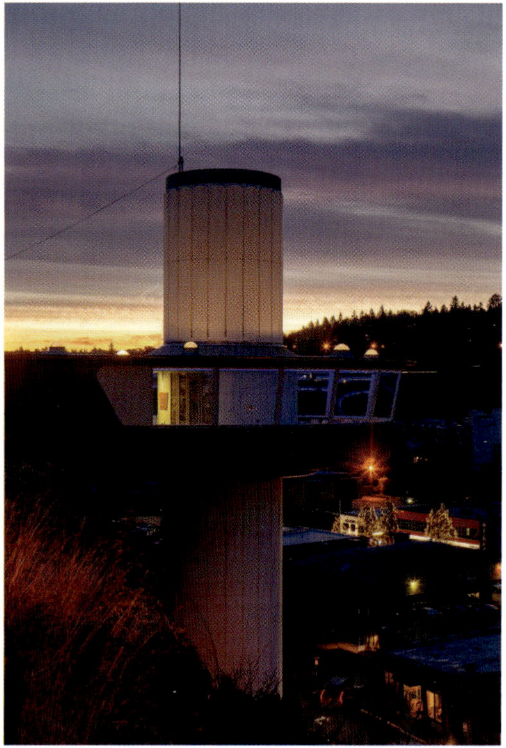

Oregon City Municipal Elevator, opened in 1915, is the only "vertical street" in North America and one of only four municipal elevators in the world. *Photo by Vldn Taylor*

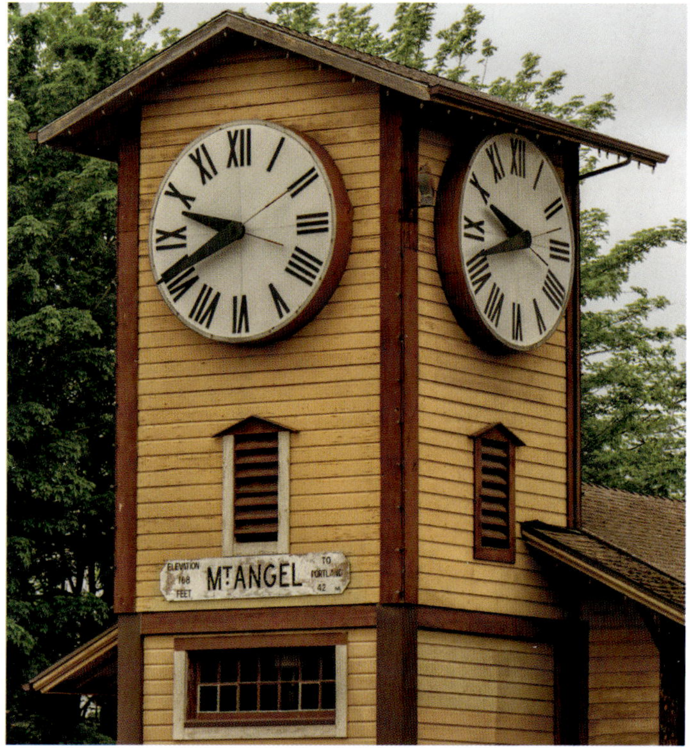

Mt. Angel railway depot. *Photo by Barbara Tricarico*

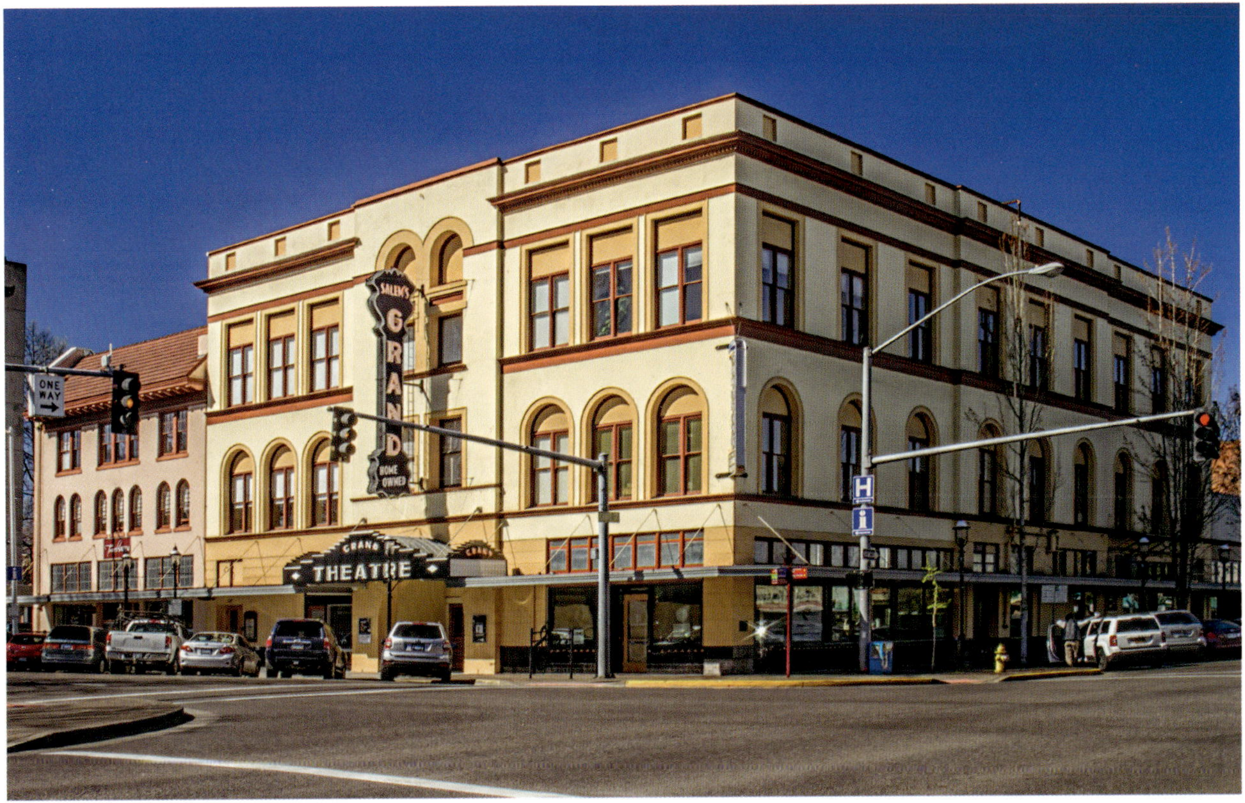

Grand Theater, Salem. Originally built in 1900 as a lodge hall and opera house by the Independent Order of Odd Fellows. *Photo by Howard Hunt*

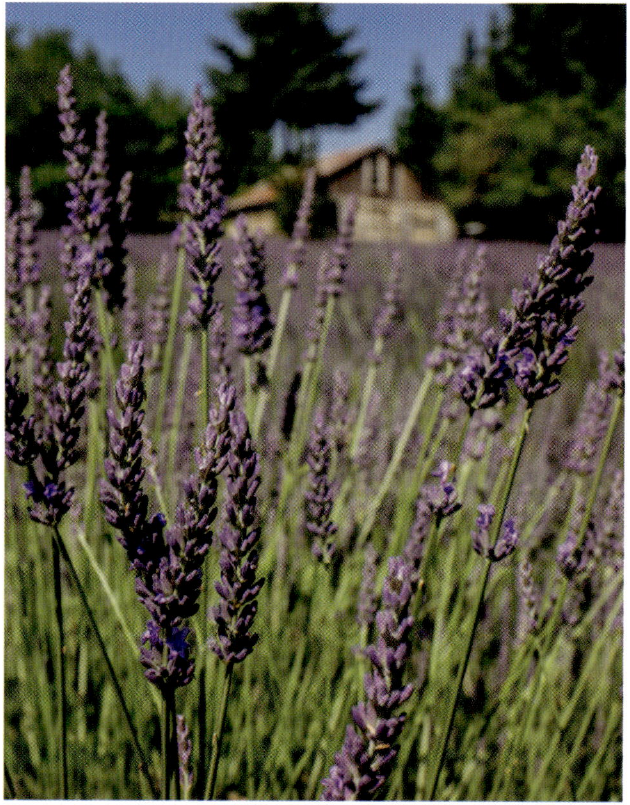

Mountainside lavender farm, Hillsboro.
Photo by Vivian McAleavey

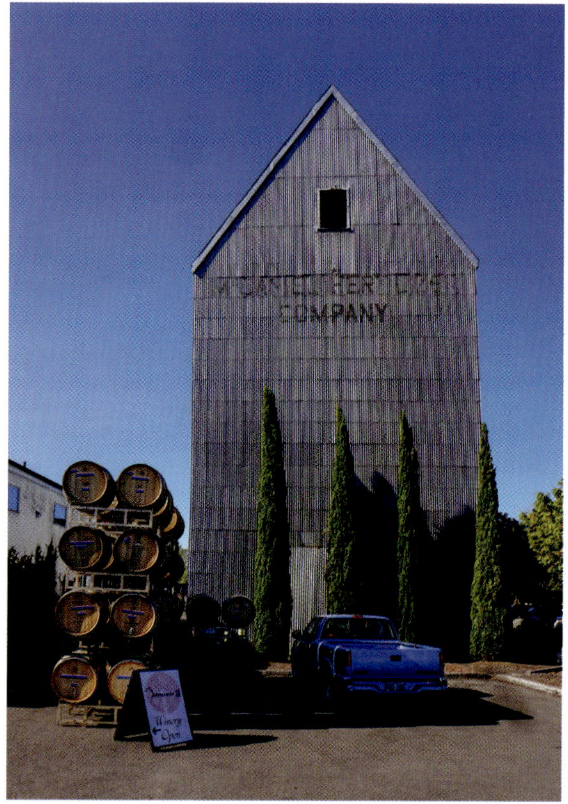

McMinnville's Historic Granary District is a cluster of former grain warehouses that house urban wineries, breweries, and shops. *Photo by Charles Hillestad*

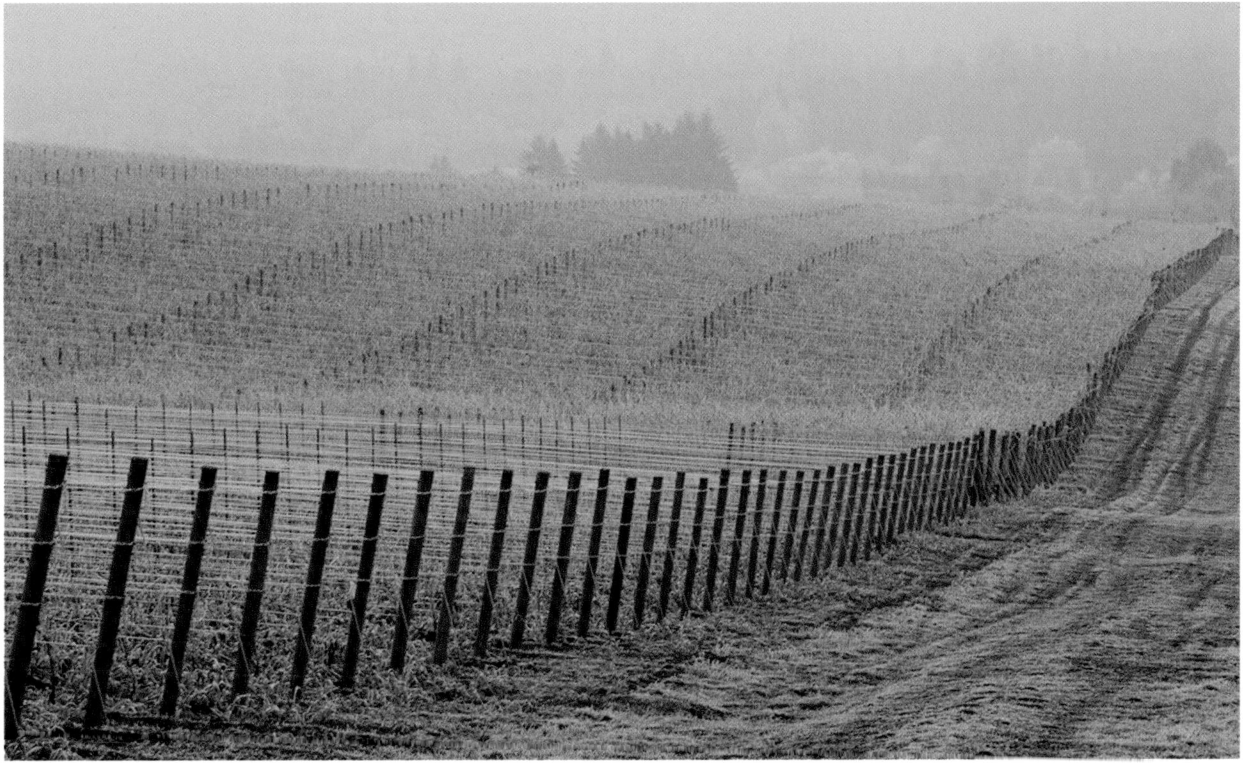

Vineyards in the mist. *Photo by Clem Paslack*

92

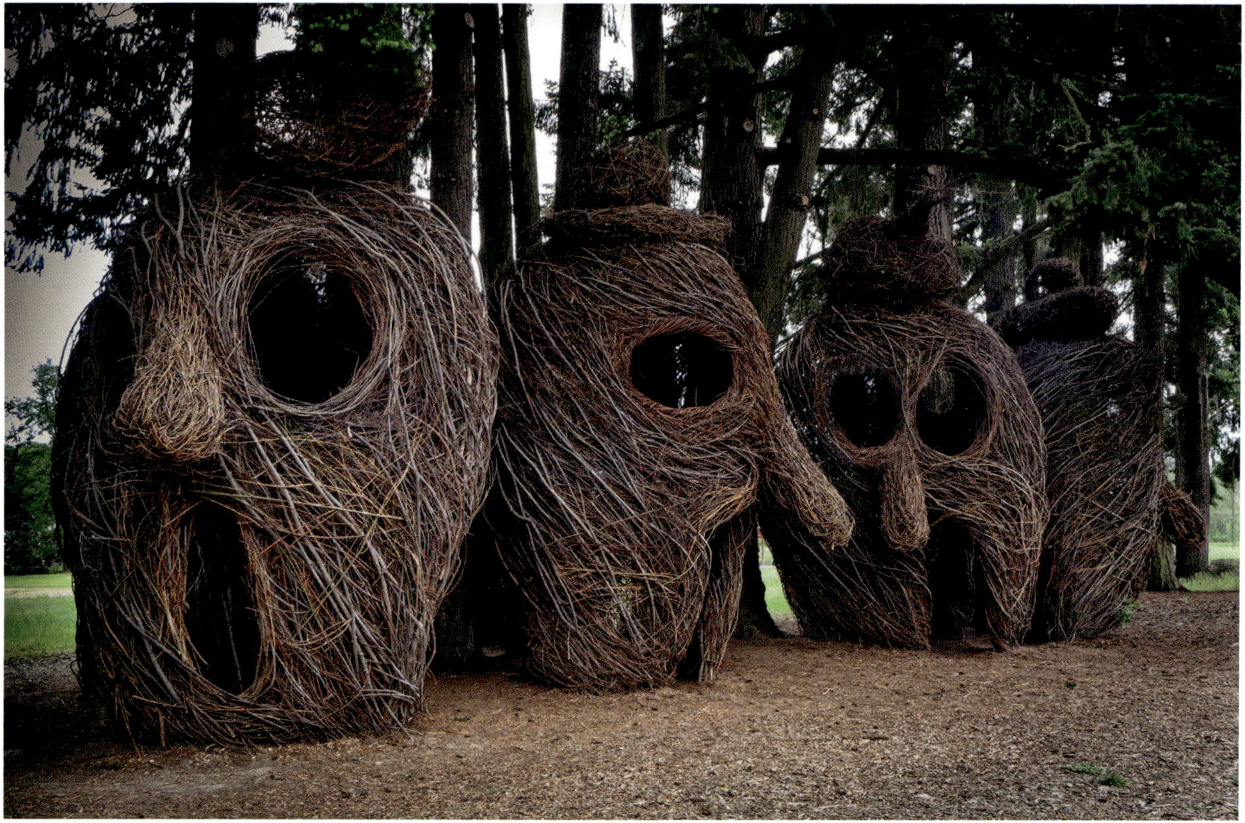

Stickwork sculptures created by artist Patrick Dougherty at Orenco Woods Nature Park, Hillsboro. *Photo by Barbara Tricarico*

Old advertising barn, Cottage Grove. *Photo by John Kirk*

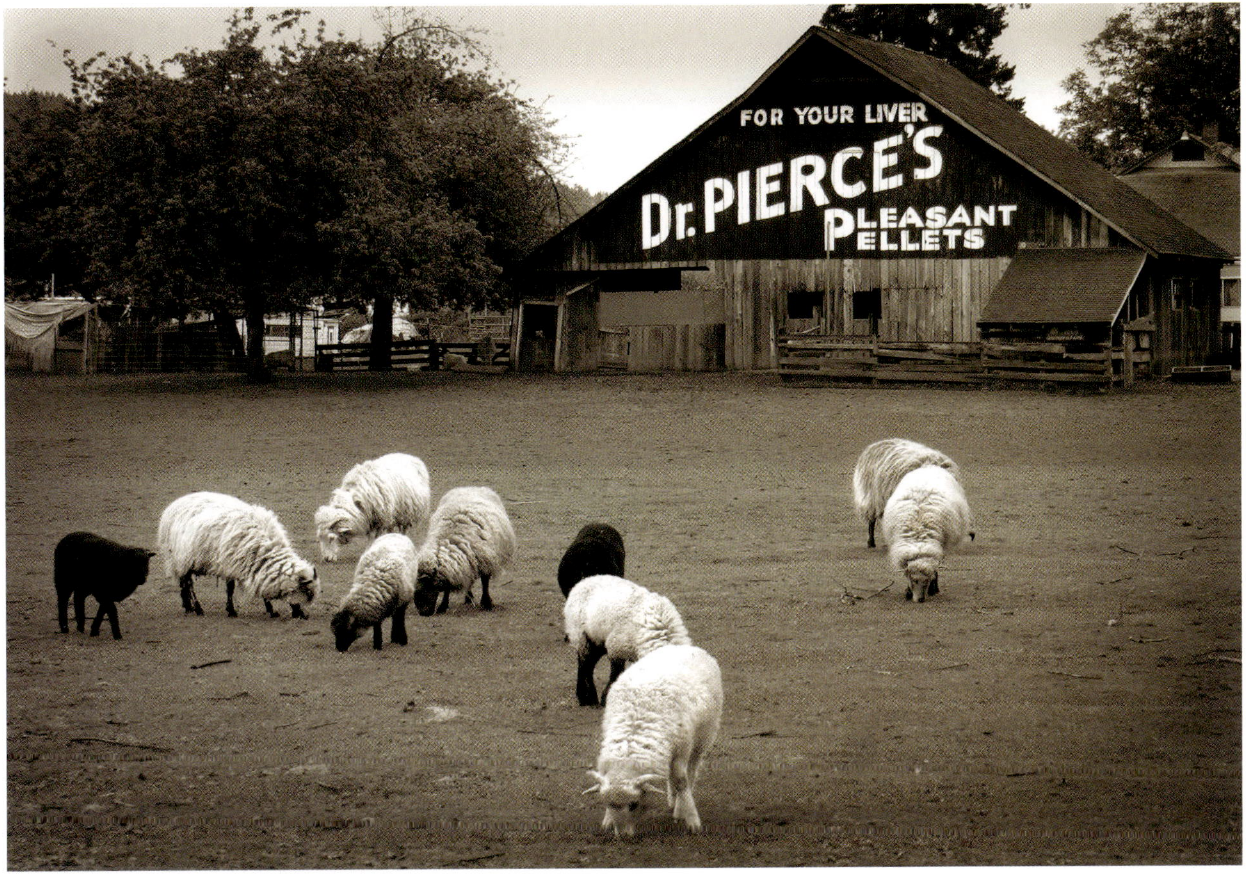
FOR YOUR LIVER
Dr. PIERCE'S
PLEASANT
PELLETS

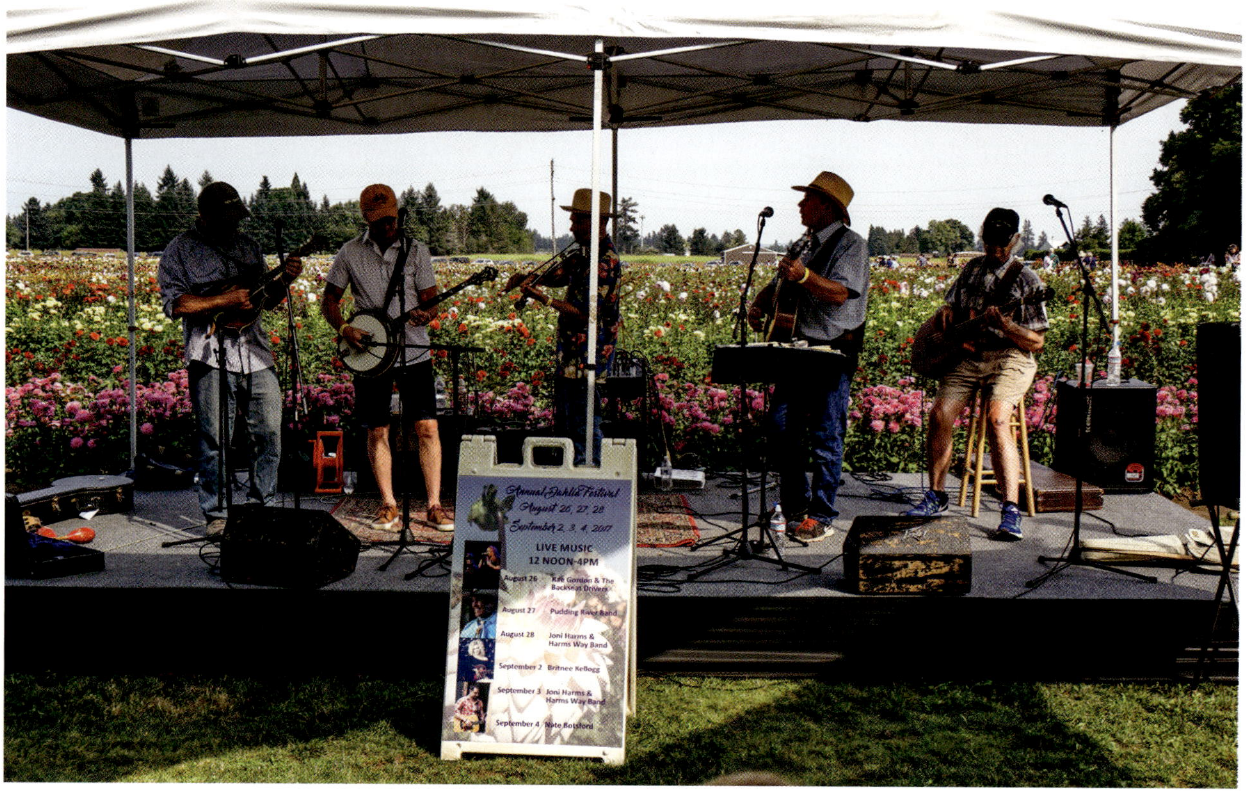

Pudding River Band performs at the Swan Island Dahlia Festival, Canby.
Photo by Charles Hillestad

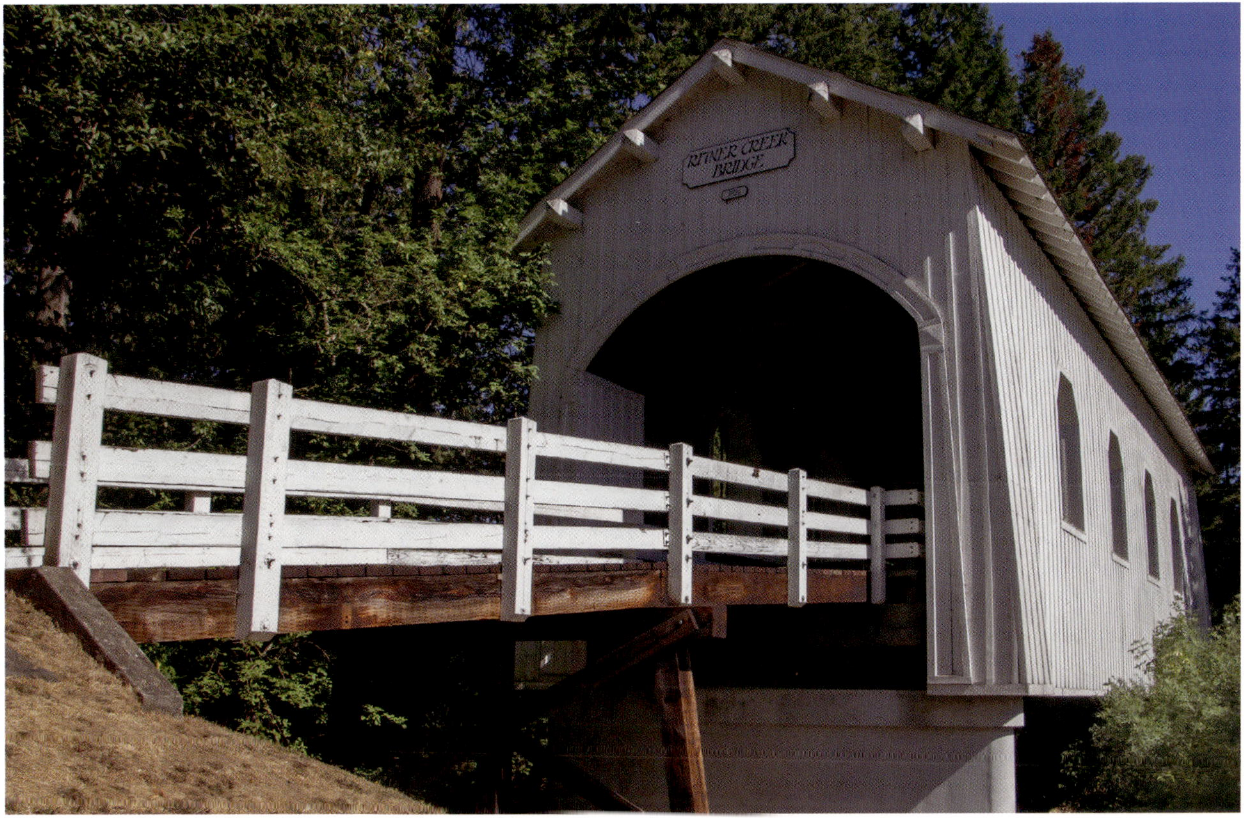

Ritner Creek Covered Bridge, Pedee, built in 1927. It was the last covered bridge on a state highway in Oregon. There are fifty historic covered bridges in the state; at one time there were approximately 450. *Photo by Diana Standing*

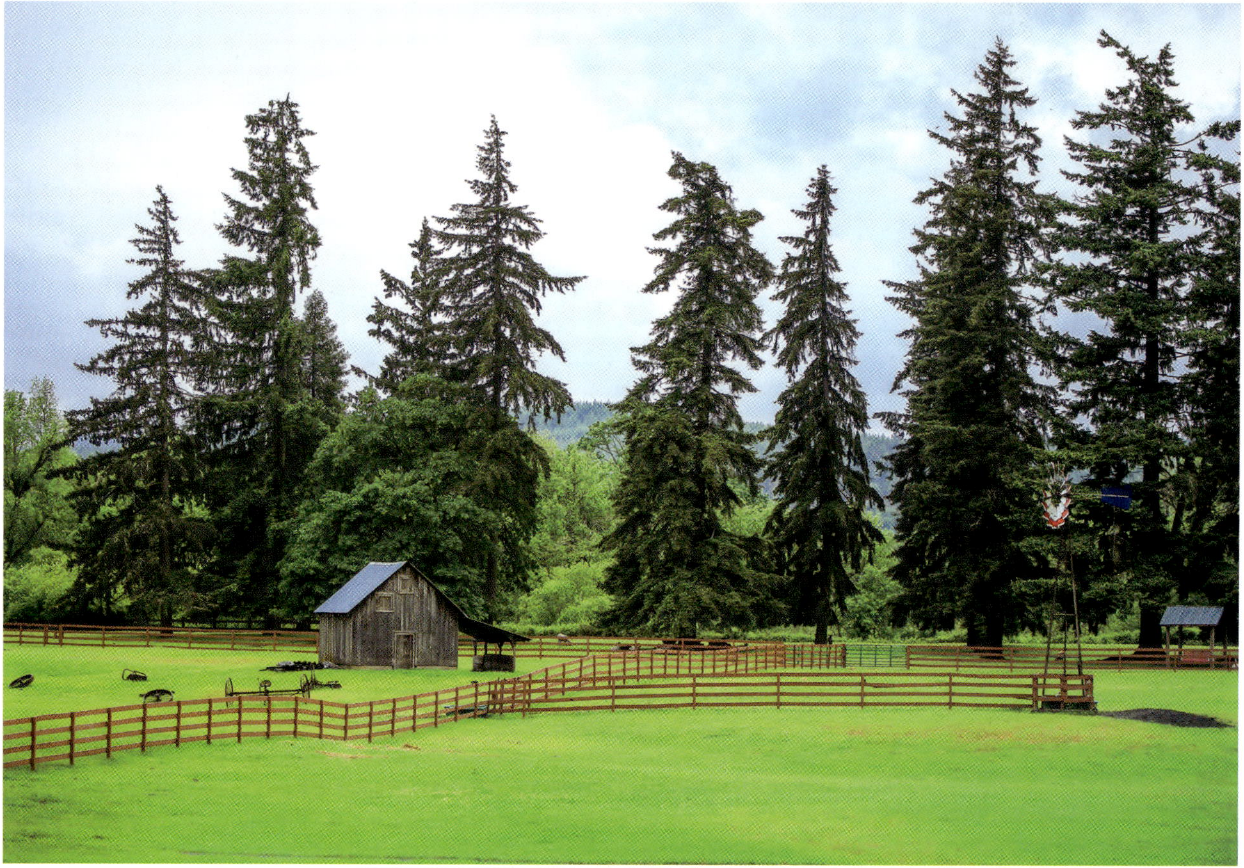

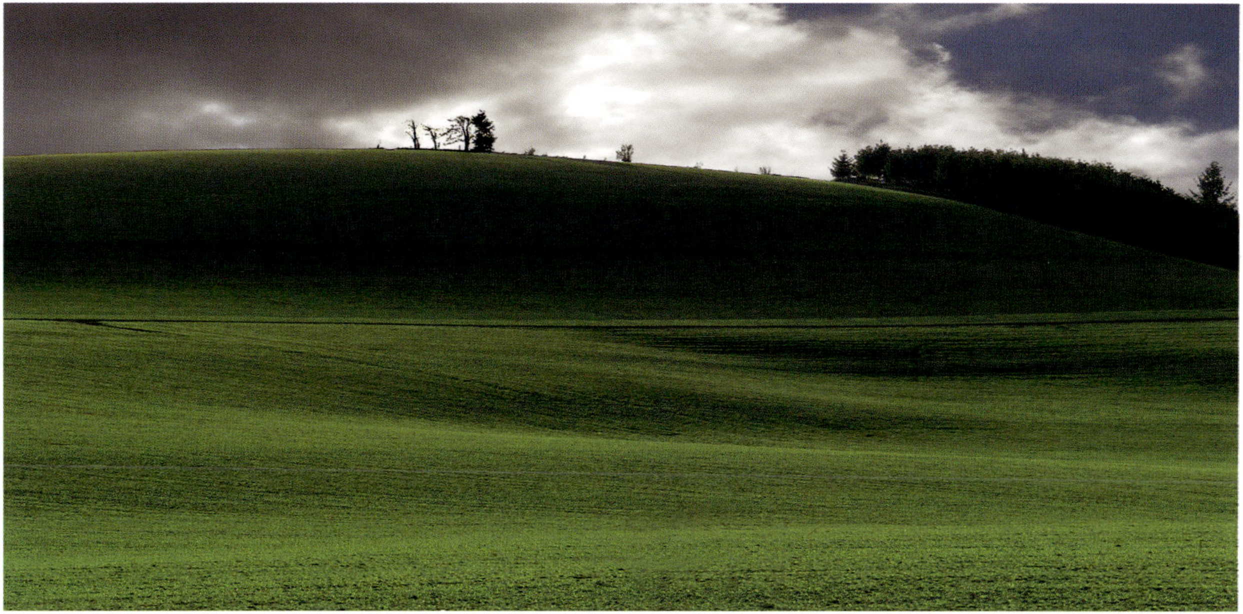

97

Farm along I-5 south of Eugene. *Photo by Terry Fisher*

Green fields near Silverton. *Photo by Charles Hillestad*

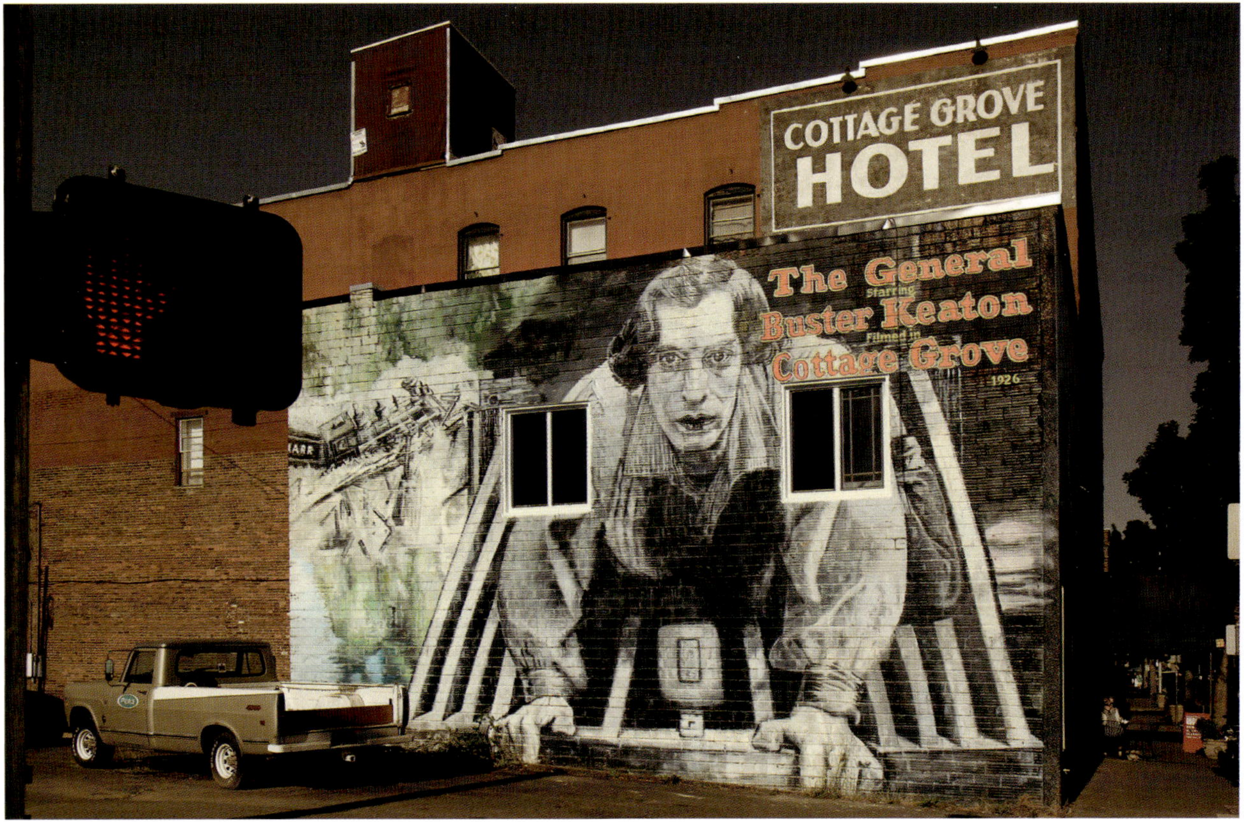

The Buster Keaton film *The General* was filmed in Cottage Grove in 1926. This mural adorns the wall of the hotel where Keaton and the film crew stayed. *Photo by John Kirk*

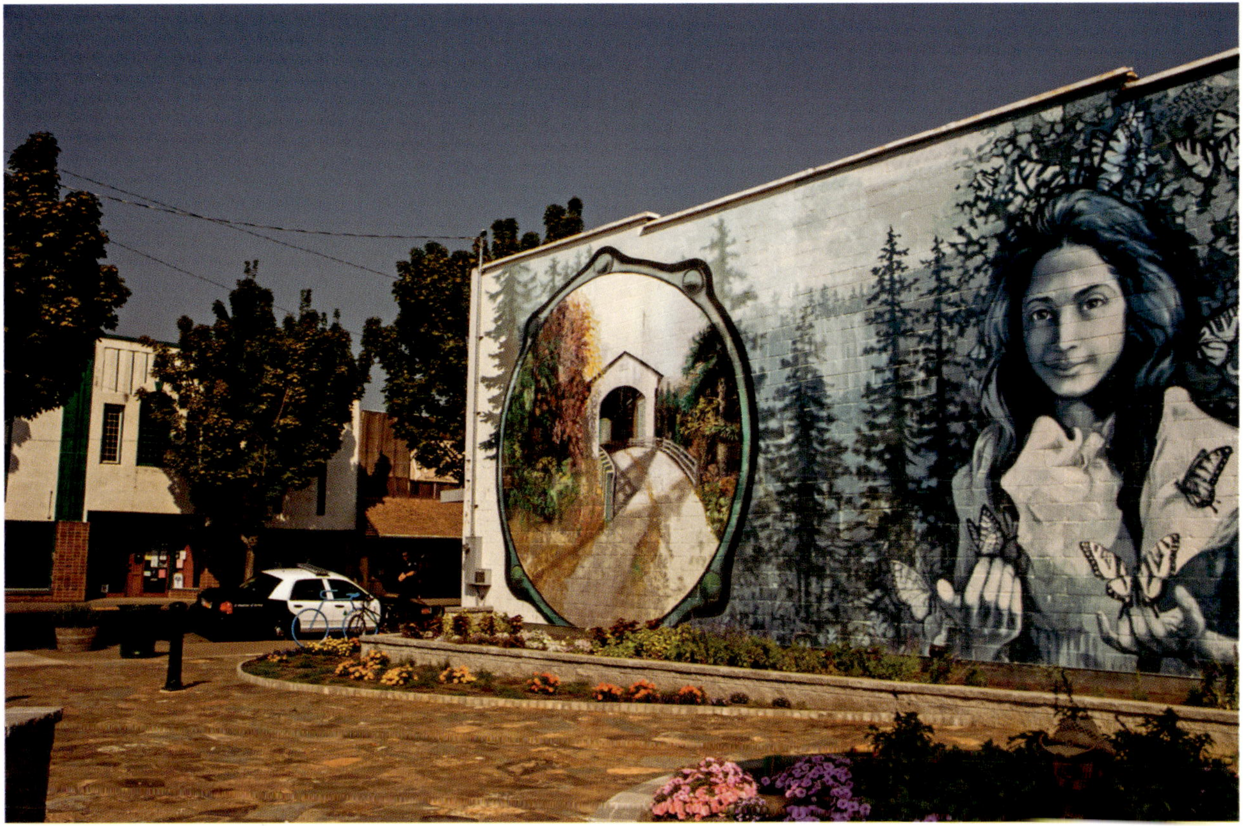

Cottage Grove mural of Opal Whiteley, one of approximately twenty in the city. *Photo by Jay Newman*

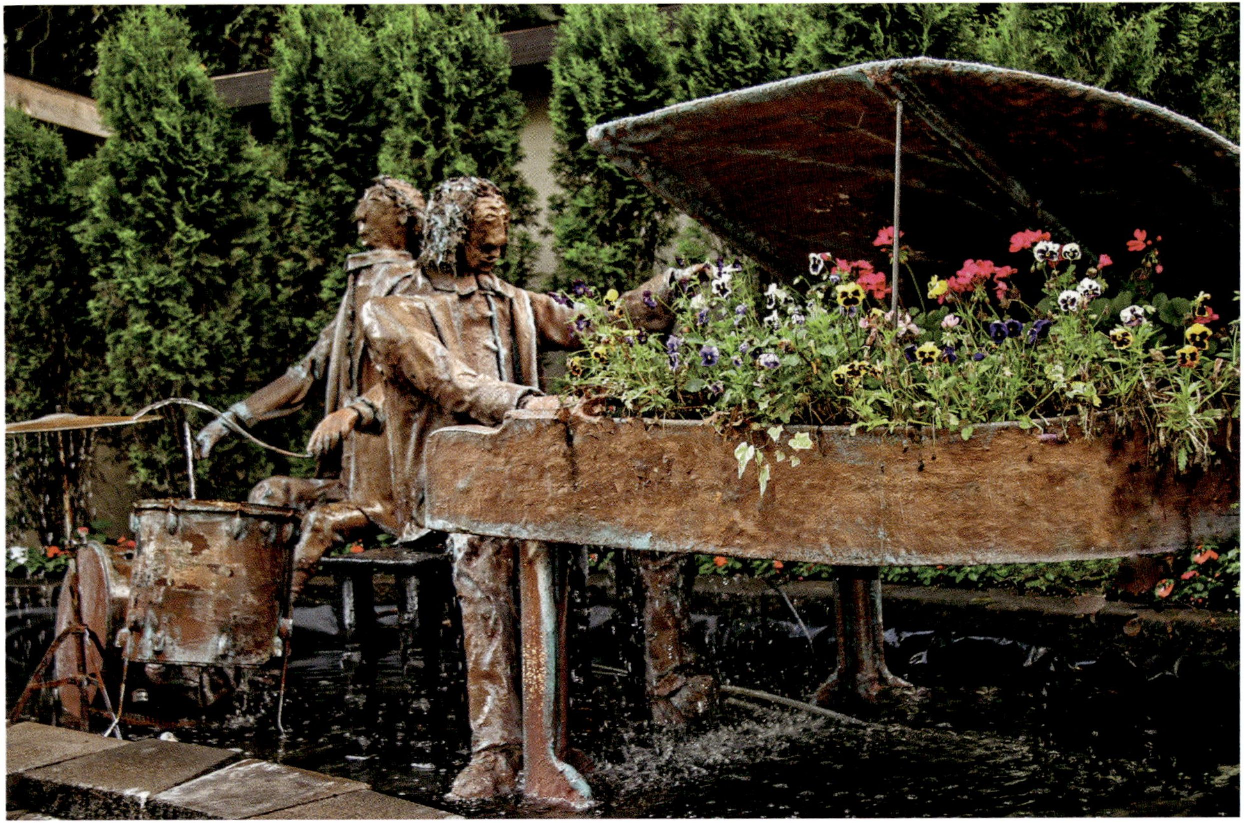

Water sculpture at Belknap Hot Springs Lodge. *Photo by Kate Geary*

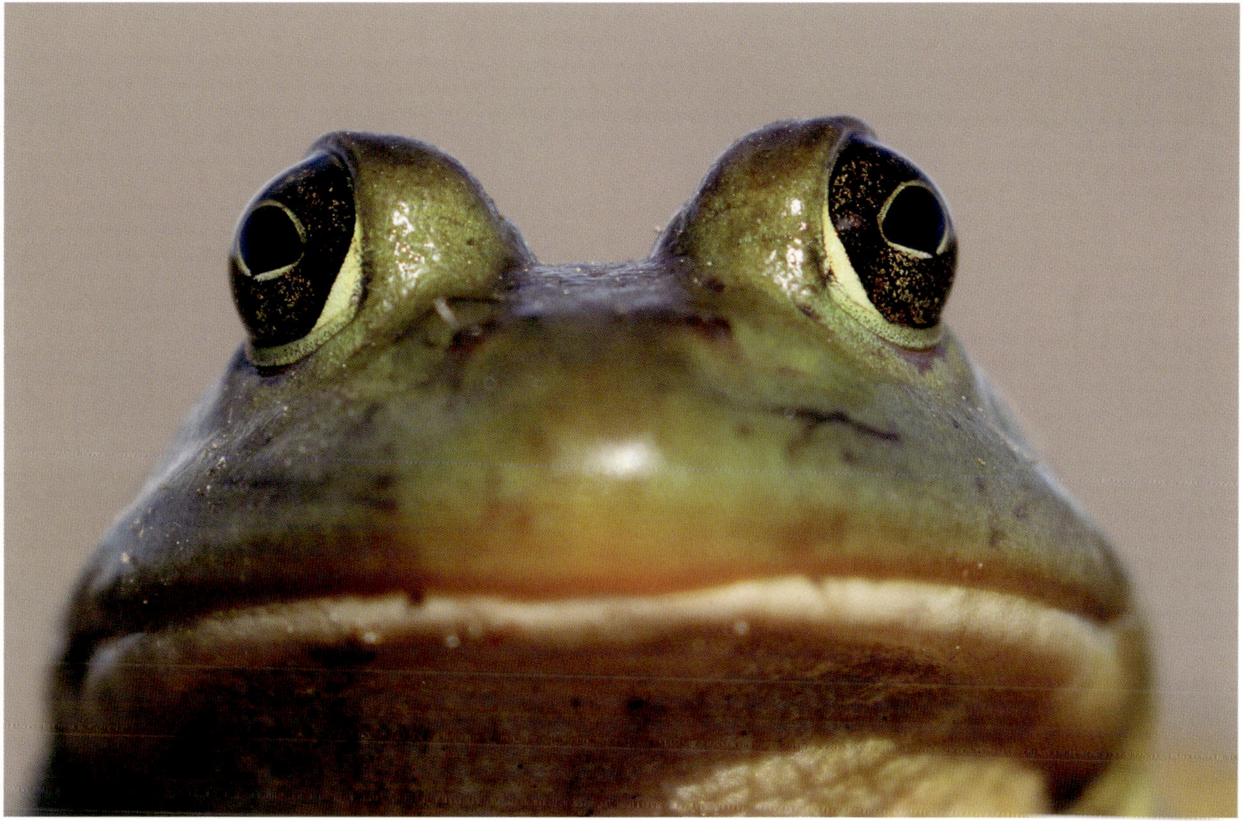

Bullfrog. *Photo by Dan Elster*

101

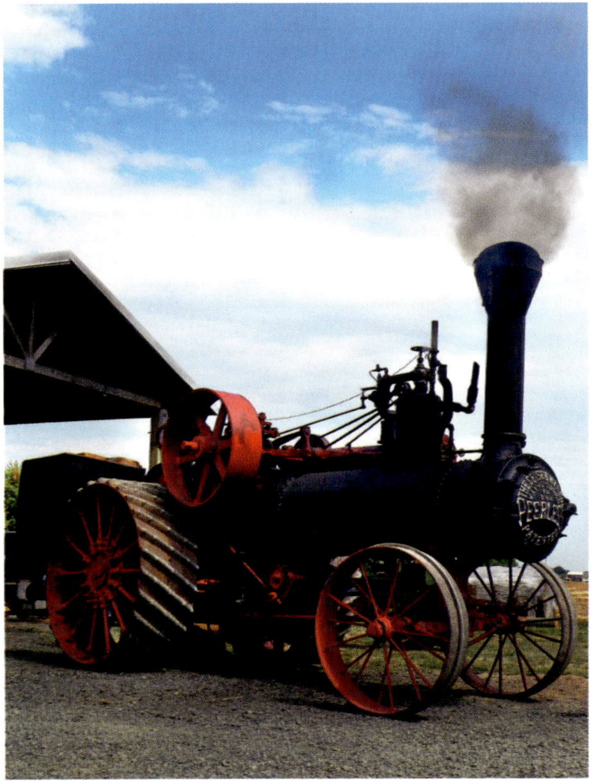

Peerless steam tractor, Yamhill Valley Heritage Center.
Photo by Charles Hillestad

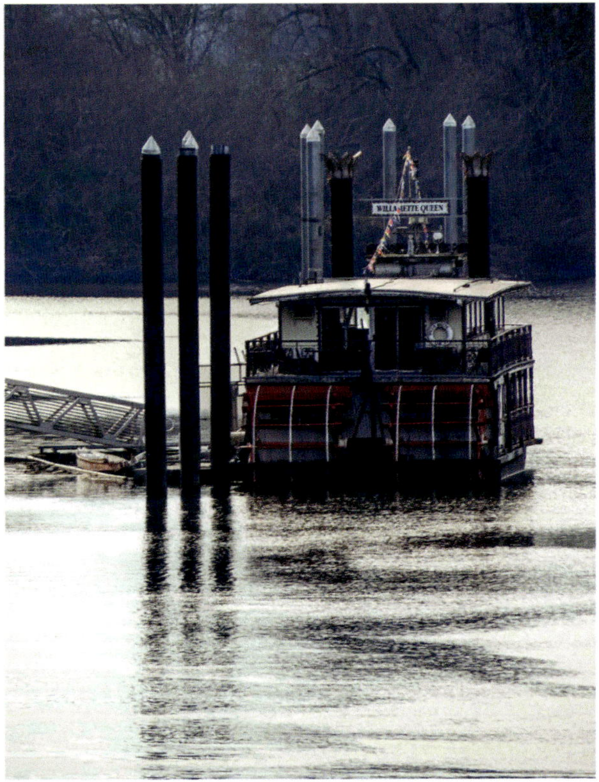

The *Willamette Queen* riverboat. *Photo by Charles Hillestad*

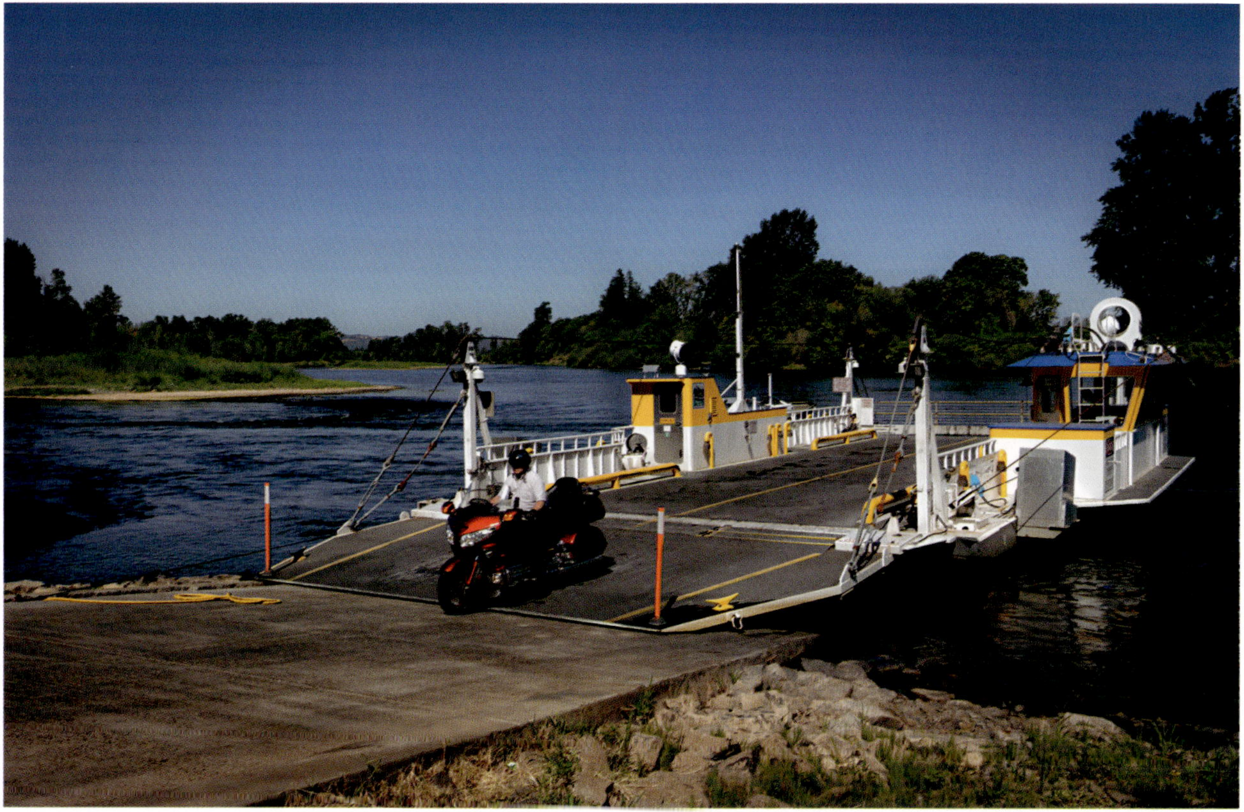

The Buena Vista Ferry connects Marion and Polk Counties. This cable ferry over the Willamette River has operated since 1852 and is one of only three ferries still running in the state. *Photo by Barbara Tricarico*

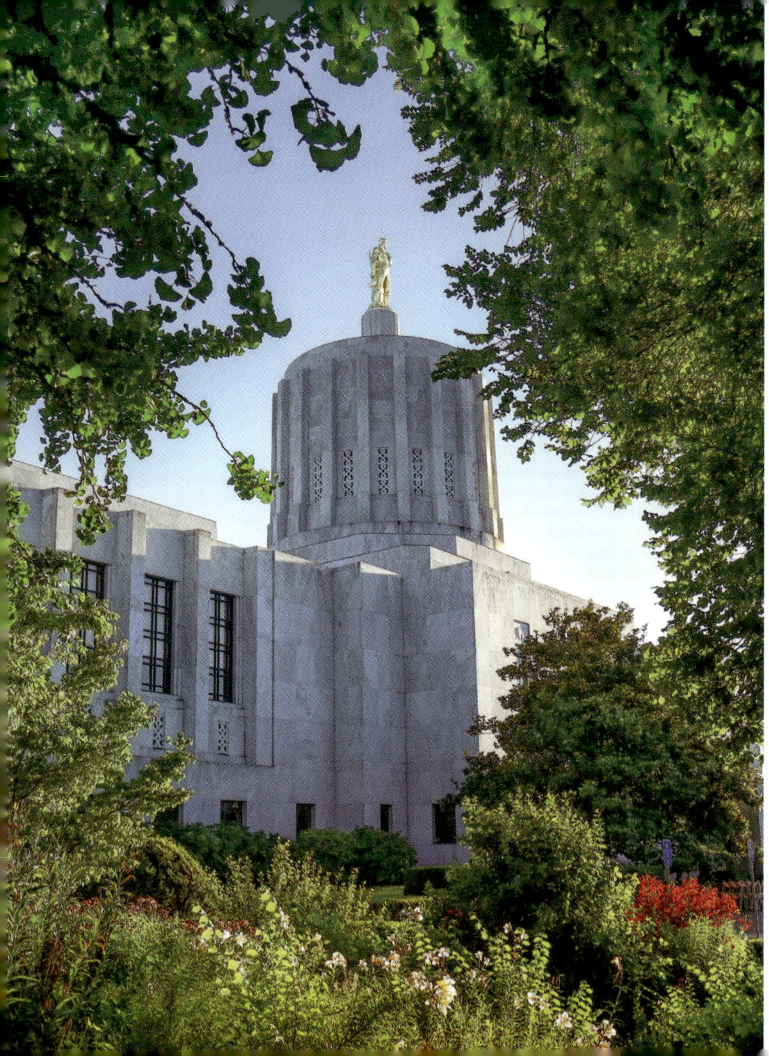

Oregon State Capitol, Salem.
Photo by Terry Fisher

The bronze and gold leaf *Oregon Pioneer* statue atop the Oregon State Capitol was created by Ulric Ellerhusen and installed in 1938. It stands 22 feet tall and weighs 8½ tons. *Photo by Charles Hillestad*

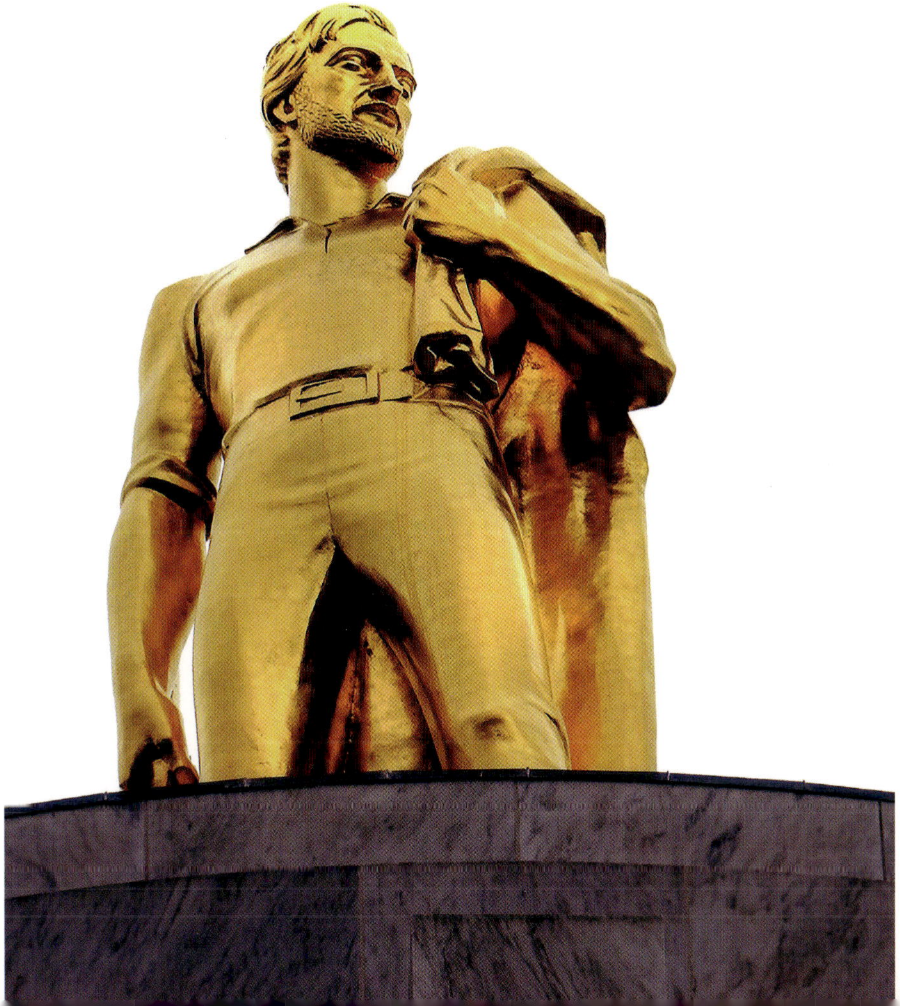

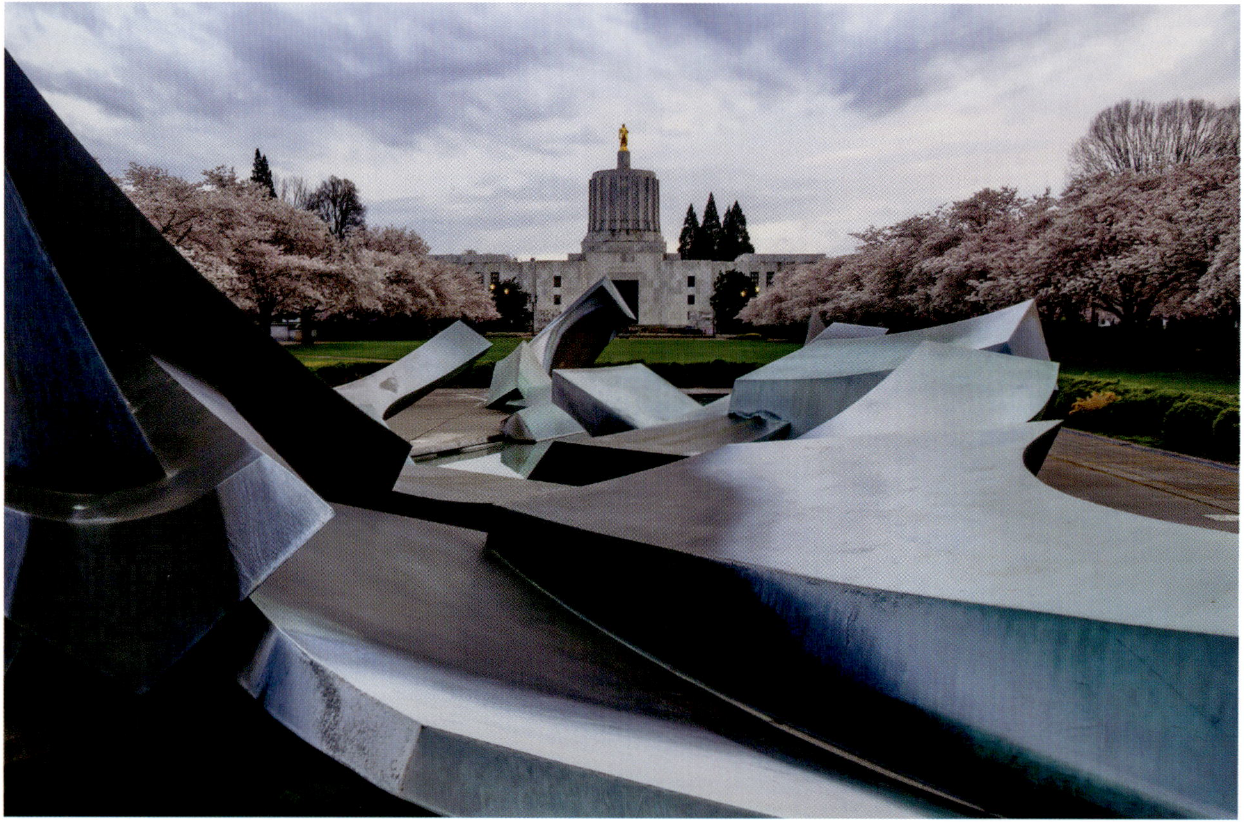

Sprague Fountain at the Oregon State Capitol, Salem.
Photo by Vldn Taylor

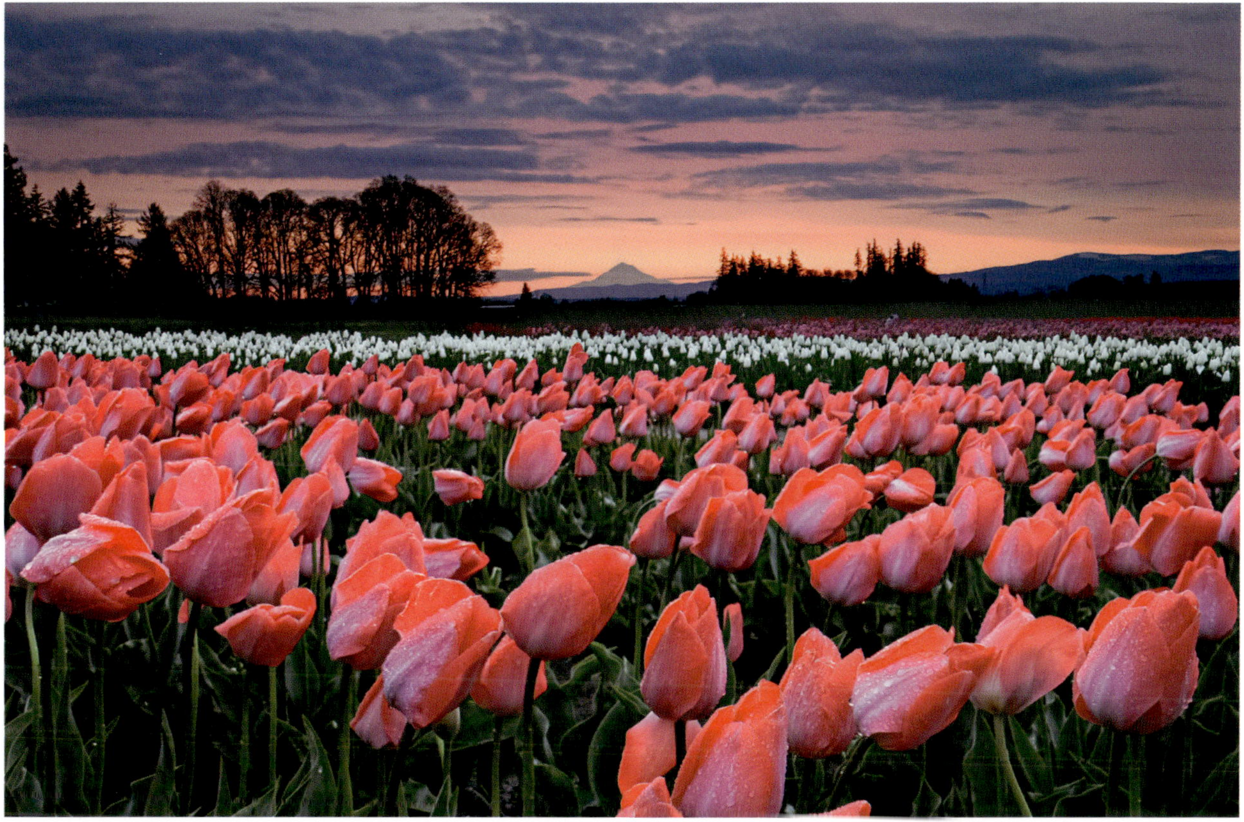

Wooden Shoe Tulip Farm, Woodburn. Mt. Hood in background.
Photo by Vldn Taylor

108

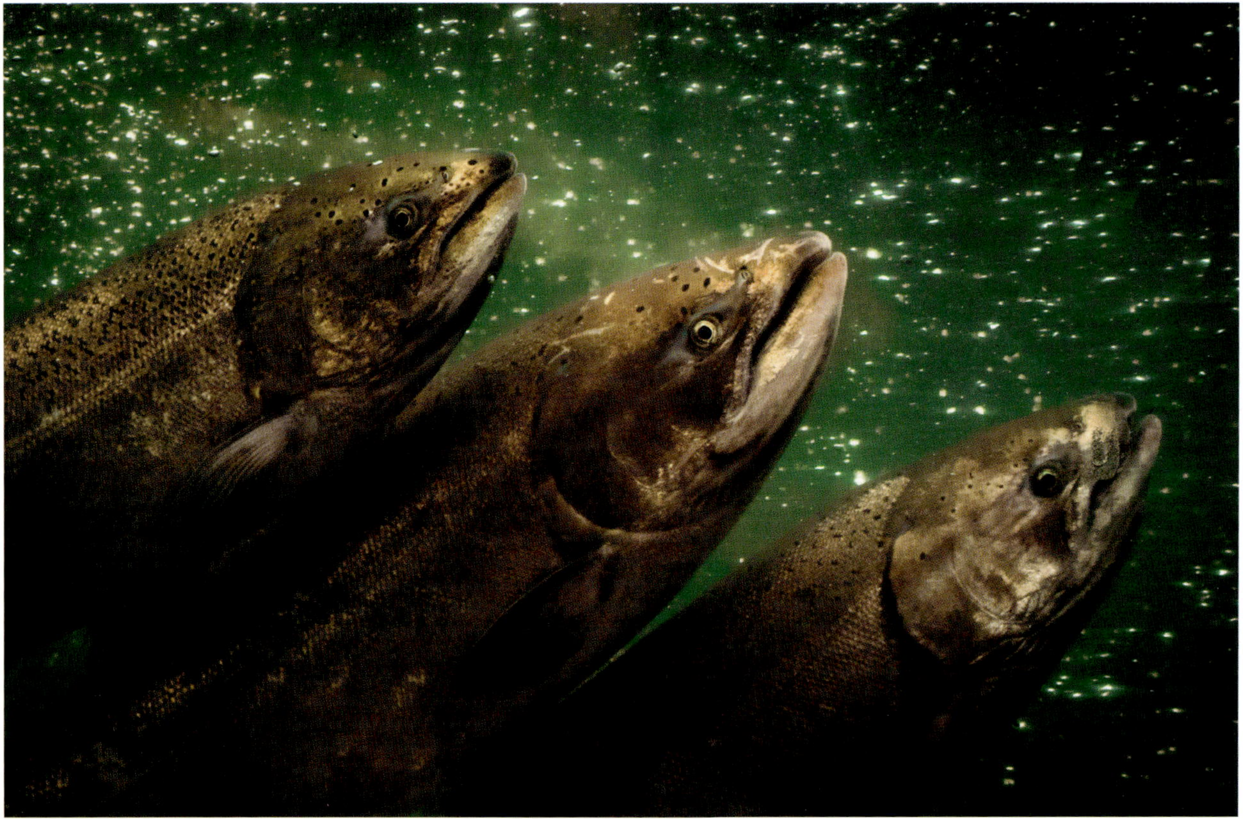

Viewing window at Winchester Dam, Roseburg.
Photo by Linda Rodgers

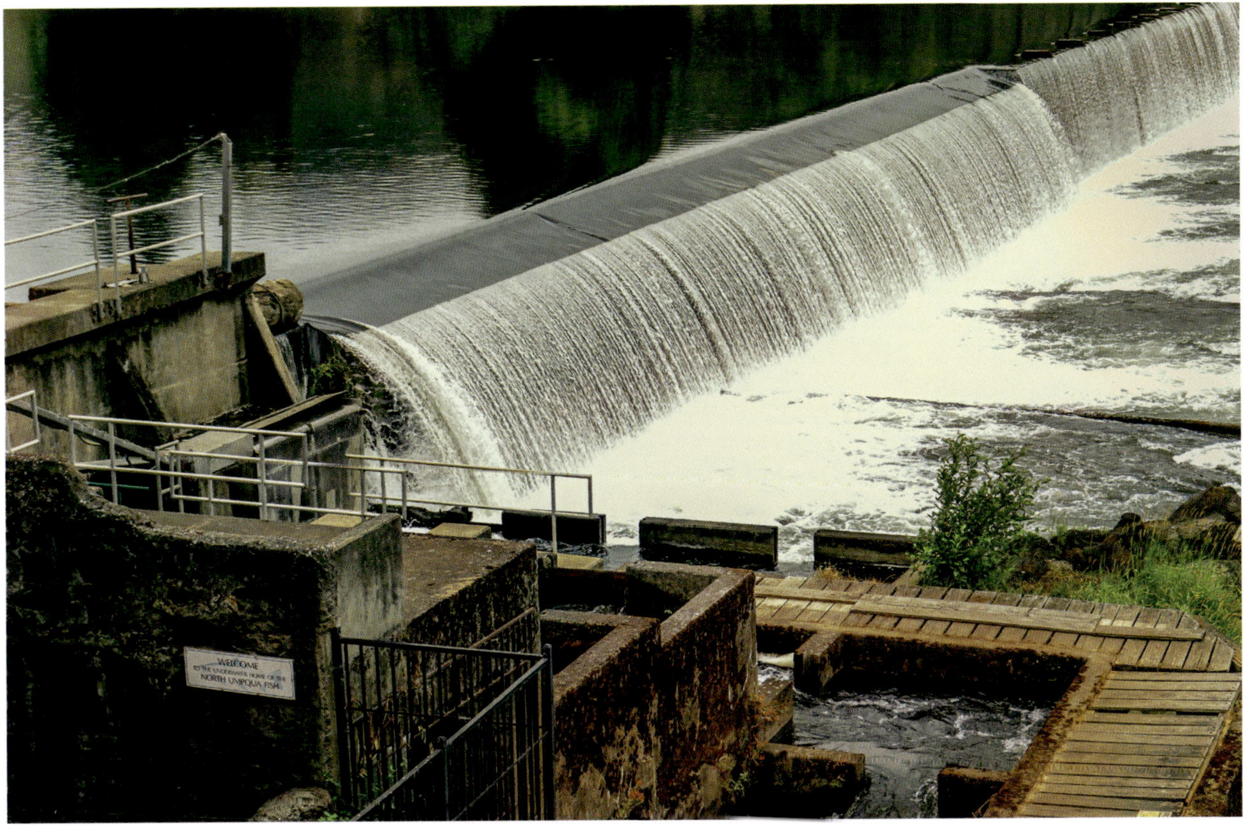

Winchester Dam, Roseburg, was built in 1890.
Photo by Cornelius Matteo

109

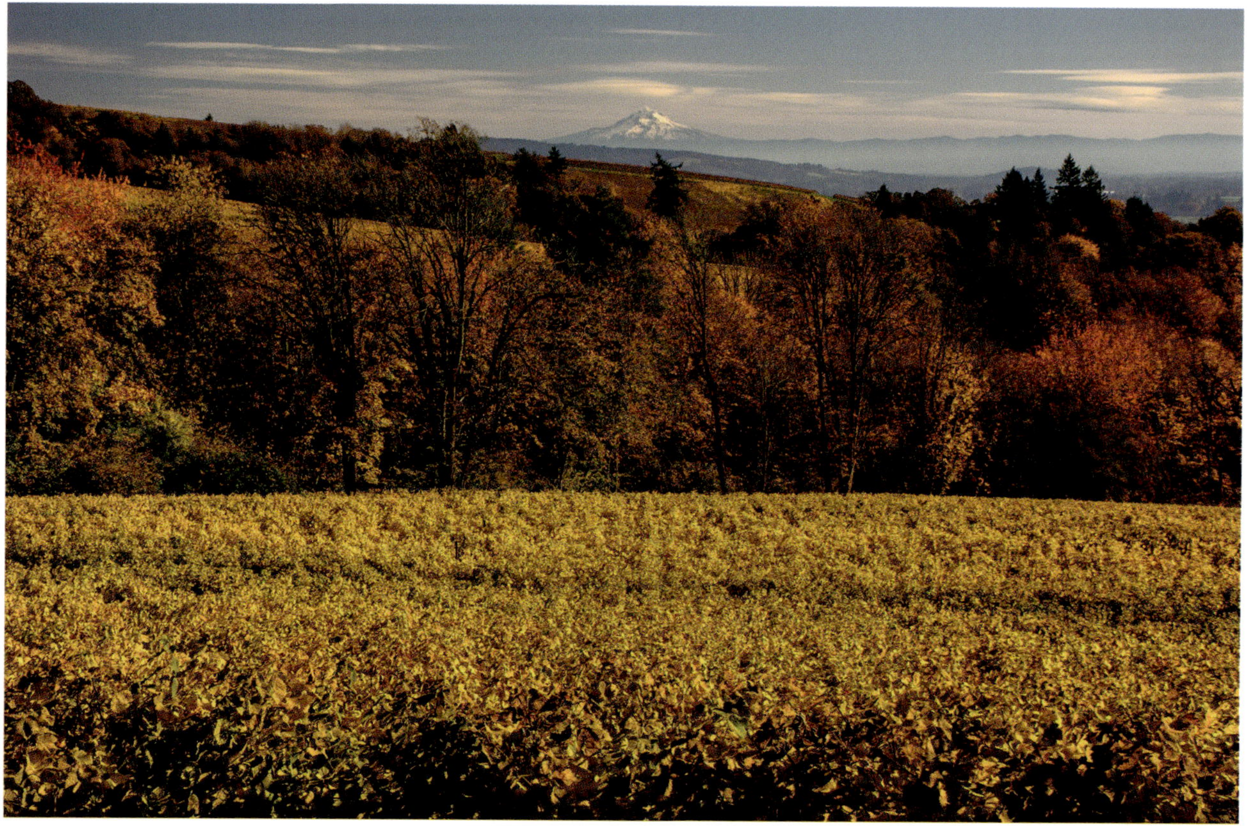

Dundee Hills in autumn, with Mt. Hood in the background. *Photo by Clem Paslack*

CREDITS

Thank you to the following Oregon photographers who contributed to this book:

Ellen Ahern
Julie Bonney
Dan Elster
Terry Fisher
Kate Geary
Gary Hill
Charles Hillestad
Howard Hunt
John Kirk
Richard Krieger
Cornelius Matteo
Vivian McAleavey
Jay Newman
Sue Newman
Bob Palermini
Clem Paslack
John Christer Petersen
George F. Peterson
Linda Rodgers
Diana Standing
Alana Lynn Starkweather
Vldn Taylor
Neal R. Thompson
Barbara Tricarico

Author photo credit:
Cornelius Matteo

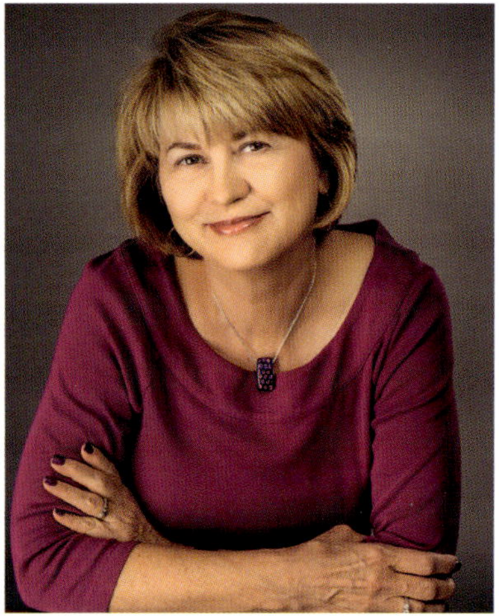

Barbara Tricarico has produced nine Oregon photography books by Schiffer, including three coffee-table books: *Oregon*; *Ashland, Oregon*; and *Ashland, Oregon Day Trips*, as well as coauthoring and photographing *Quilts of Virginia: 1607–1899*. She and her husband, Bill, moved to Ashland, Oregon, in 2010. Barbara is an active member of the Ashland Chamber of Commerce and Southern Oregon Photographic Association. She is a regular volunteer for the Ashland Food Project and the Oregon Shakespeare Festival. Barbara has traveled and photographed extensively around the world. Follow her on Facebook at Barbara Tricarico Photography or visit her website, www.barbaratricarico.com.